SOLDIER LIFE

SOLDIER LIFE

THE EDITORS OF TIME-LIFE BOOKS

ISBN-13: 978-0-7607-9033-5
ISBN-10: 0-7607-9033-7

Printed and bound in China

10 9 8 7 6 5 4 3 2 1

Contents

A WINTER ENCAMPMENT

Civil war armies marched and fought in the warm seasons and holed up over the winter. The painting depicts a typical winter camp for a Federal (or Confederate) regiment, with its assortment of tents, cabins, and log-and-canvas structures all neatly laid out according to regulation.

Noncommissioned Officers'
Quarters – Staff

Provost Marshall

Officers' Quarters –
Company

Latrines

Officers' Quarters –
Field and Staff

Baggage Train

Enlisted Men's Quarters

Stockade (Prison)

Noncommissioned Officers'
Quarters

Sutler

Noncommissioned Officers
Quarters – Staff

Answering the Call

In September of 1887 an Ohio newspaperman named Wilbur F. Hinman published a hefty 700-page account of the Civil War. The conflict had ended more than two decades earlier, but for millions of veterans like Wilbur Hinman, the memories of those four years were an indelible personal legacy, seared upon the soul. "This volume is not a history," Hinman wrote in his foreword, "nor is it a 'story' in the usual acceptation of the word." His intention was to portray, in a novelistic format, "the every-day life of the soldier" with "fidelity to the actual life of a million volunteers." Having commenced his wartime service as a 21-year-old private and emerged a battle-scarred lieutenant colonel, Hinman drew upon his own abundant experience in the ranks of the 65th Ohio Infantry to present a truthful record of how he and his comrades "lived and talked, and what they did and suffered"—the mixture of "mirth and profanity" that was soldier life.

Though not a bestseller in the traditional sense, *Corporal Si Klegg and His "Pard"* gained a wide readership among the veterans of the war—so much so that the leading Union veterans paper, the *National Tribune*, ran no fewer than eight sequels to the story. Much of the book's success was due to the honest portrayal of soldiering as seen through the eyes of Hinman's protagonist, a teenage Ohio farmer named Josiah Klegg.

Like so many other naive young men lured to war by fifes and drums and patriotic entreaties, Si had seen nothing of the great world that lay beyond his farm. But his introduction to military service was not the adventure that he anticipated. For all his dreams of glory, he quickly found himself "but an atom of the mighty army," and an insignificant one at that. He was issued an ill-fitting uniform coat that reached to his ankles and a knapsack he soon filled "with an endless variety of useless things." Woefully ignorant of drill, he handled his musket "very much as he would a hoe," and for all he knew "a 'platoon' might

Soldiers of the Port Gibson Rifles, a company of the 10th Mississippi Infantry, pose in March 1861 for photographer J. D. Edwards at Camp Davis, their pine-shaded bivouac near Fort Barrancas on Pensacola Bay. A British correspondent described these men as "great long-bearded fellows in flannel shirts and slouched hats."

be something to eat." As they chuckled at Si Klegg's misadventures, many veterans no doubt recalled their own awkward initiation into the realities of army life.

Like thousands of other fledgling warriors, Si Klegg began to learn the ins and outs of soldiering from an older and wiser comrade who had already "seen the elephant"—the soldiers' euphemism for the baptism of fire. Si's friend and tentmate—or "pard" in army slang—was a lean and grizzled volunteer named Shorty, a man "not dazzled by the splendor of martial glory." With patience and gentle humor Shorty helped the stocky young farm boy to abandon his "sentimental notions" and to "sink the individual in the soldier." Under Shorty's tutelage Si learned how to grind coffee beans with a bayonet, how to soften and fry the "cast-iron" hardtack biscuits, how to forage for chickens and pigs when officers were not looking, and how to make do with a simple blanket roll rather than the bulky knapsack. And, perhaps most important of all, Shorty taught Si Klegg to be "cheerful and even mirthful . . . in the presence of death."

Tested in battle and rewarded with promotion to corporal, Si Klegg possessed a strong constitution and indomitable pluck, qualities that enabled him to survive wounds and imprisonment and return to his farm a wiser man, "a veteran—a soldier, in the fullest significance of the word," and "conscious that he had acted well his part." But like so many other veterans of that war, Si had endured the pain of irreparable loss with the death of his pard, Shorty.

"The ties that bound near comrades and associates in the army were more than those of friendship," Wilbur Hinman wrote. His own pard—Private Wilbur Hulet—had fallen

in the Battle of Chickamauga, and it was to his memory that Hinman dedicated *Si Klegg,* noting, "We slept under the same blanket, and drank from the same canteen." The poignant sentiment was one no veteran could fail to recognize, and it stirred memories none would ever forget.

Some three million Americans took up arms during the four years of the Civil War, with Northern armies holding a more than 2-to-1 advantage in numbers over their Southern opponents. Although cumulative statistics are incomplete for the Union and lacking altogether for the Confederacy, existing records show that the typical Federal volunteer bore many similarities to Si Klegg. It was a young man's war, with 18-year-olds composing the largest single age group at enlistment and 98.5 percent of soldiers falling between the ages of 18 and 45. The average Yankee recruit was a 25-year-old farmer who stood five feet, eight and one-quarter inches tall, weighed 143 pounds, and had dark hair, blue eyes, and a light complexion.

Farmers made up 48 percent of the Federal enlistees, mechanics 24 percent, laborers 16 percent, with eight percent in commercial or professional pursuits. Lacking the industrial base of the North, Southern armies fielded a higher percentage of farmers, while Union forces contained a greater number of recruits from urban areas. Many more Federals than Confederates were foreign born, principally Irish and Germans who had settled in cities such as New York, Philadelphia, Boston, and Chicago. Nonetheless it is safe to assume that the typical Rebel was, statistically speaking, much the same as his Yankee counterpart.

Similar as they were in age, appearance, and occupation, however, these men had

been forced by decades of sectional divisiveness into two armed camps, separated by irreconcilable differences and a conflicting vision of what their nation was meant to be. Each side cherished the certain conviction that its cause was just. "I never entertained a doubt as to the South having the best of the Constitutional argument," recalled Robert Stiles, a Yale graduate who left Connecticut to fight for his native Virginia. "I believed firmly my people in the South were right; I knew well they were weak; I saw clearly they were about to be invaded." He concluded that the stand he was taking against Northern tyranny and aggression stemmed from "the God-implanted instinct which impels a man to *defend his own hearth-stone.*"

Confederates saw a parallel between their struggle for the right to secede from a tyrannical government and the ideals that inspired the revolutionary founders of the republic. Carlton McCarthy, who enlisted with Stiles in an artillery unit known as the Richmond Howitzers, felt it incumbent upon every Southerner—"having assumed for himself a nationality"—to pledge "his sacred honor" to the Confederacy. Marylander William McKim saw the Confederacy as representing "the sacred right of self-government," and its defenders as battling "in vindication of the principles enunciated in the Declaration of Independence." General Robert E. Lee frequently evoked that heritage of patriotism to galvanize his troops. "Soldiers!" Lee proclaimed, "You tread, with no unequal steps, the road by which your fathers marched through suffering, privation, and blood to independence!"

At the heart of the impassioned debate, dissentious wrangling, and mutual threats of force that preceded the outbreak of the Civil

War lay the South's symbiotic relationship with the "peculiar institution" of slavery. But while Northern abolitionists on the one hand, and Southern "fire-eaters" on the other, were irreconcilably divided along pro- and anti-slavery lines, the great majority of citizens—Northern and Southern alike—were largely ambivalent toward the fate of black Americans. Confederates pointed to the fact that most Southerners did not own or traffic in slaves. Upon inquiry, one Louisianan discovered that of the 86 soldiers in his company only 31 had any direct connection to the institution.

Although he was defensive of slavery as an economic necessity, James Johnston Pettigrew—an author and intellectual who would rise to general's rank in the Confederate service—decried the radicalism of extremists on both sides of the issue. For Pettigrew the broader issue was one of cultural and philosophical differences that pitted an increasingly industrialized North against the agricultural, Arcadian South. Pettigrew believed that Northerners in general, and New Englanders in particular, represented "a civilization which reduces men to machines, which sacrifices half that is stalwart and individual to humanity to the false glitter of centralization, and to the luxurious enjoyments of a manufacturing, money age!"

While emancipation was not a primary motivation for most Northern recruits, some saw slavery as a curse of biblical proportions. "Four millions of human beings are suffering under the chain and the lash," wrote Illinois volunteer Orson Young; "we are now paying the price of our national sin." In accepting the presentation of a sword from his friends in Albany, James C. Rice of the 44th New York Infantry declared, "It is God's divine purpose, having used the wrath of the South

to commence this war, to cause that wrath to praise Him by the freedom of every slave."

The vast majority of Yankee volunteers were impelled to take up arms not from a hatred of slavery but from a belief in the integrity of the republic. Pennsylvania officer Frederick L. Hitchcock believed that by vanquishing the militant proponents of states rights, the North would "save to liberty and freedom the life of the best government the world ever saw." Bidding farewell to his family, Ohioan George H. Cadman noted, "I want you to remember that it will be not only for my country and children, but for liberty all over the world that I risked my life; for if liberty should be crushed here, what hope would there be for the cause of human progress anywhere else?"

Many immigrants who had fled oppression and found a better life in America linked their family's future with the preservation of the Union. Irish-born James McKay Rorty had worked for four years to raise enough funds to bring his parents and nine siblings to Manhattan. With most of his family still in Donegal, Rorty justified his enlistment in the Federal army in a letter to his father, writing that the "separation of this Union into North and South would not only be fatal to the progress of constitutional freedom but would put impassable barriers in the way of future immigration." Rorty further asserted, "Our only guarantee is the Constitution, our only safety is in the Union, one, and indivisible."

When war broke out in April 1861, young men on both sides of the Mason-Dixon line found themselves swept away in a tide of idealistic fervor. New Yorker Thomas Southwick, a staunch Democrat who had voted against Abraham Lincoln in the election of 1860, decided to sign up when he saw a local

militia unit parading down Broadway. "There was something thrilling in the thought that these brave young fellows were going to battle bravely for what they believed to be right," Southwick recalled. And when he caught sight of "the glorious old flag," carried by a stalwart color sergeant, Southwick's mind was made up. "I shouted and yelled until I was hoarse. Tears gushed into my eyes and I turned away firmly resolved to defend that flag against any that would raise their hands against it, whether they were my countrymen or not."

"Excitement was at white heat," noted John W. Stevens, a Confederate recruit from Texas; "our patriotism was just bubbling up and boiling over and frying and fizzling." As the bands played "Dixie" and "The Bonnie Blue Flag," Virginian Fannie Beers joined other loyal Southern women in helping to outfit their departing loved ones with natty new uniforms. "The Confederate gray was then a thing of beauty," she remembered, "the outer garb of true and noble souls. Every man who wore it became ennobled in the eyes of every woman." With units being organized under the auspices of their respective states, and most recruits hailing from the same town or county, some men enlisted so as not to appear malingerers in the eyes of their friends and neighbors. As Richmonder Carlton McCarthy put it, "To stay was dishonor and shame!"

Not all volunteers were motivated by patriotism, political convictions, or regional pride. John Haley signed on with the 17th Maine looking for "a change," and from "an overwhelming desire to see the country." Others, like Michigan lawyer Charles B. Haydon, thought the dangers of active service would be preferable to the stifling routine of civil life. "I know the Law which I loved so much would have killed me," Haydon reflected. "If I should fall during the war I shall be sure of having turned my life to good account." Convinced from his reading of swashbuckling novels "that war was a glorious thing," 17-year-old John N. Opie left his studies to join the 5th Virginia "without, at the time, being able to give a reasonable why or wherefore."

Once they had made the determination to enlist, many volunteers sought to convince their families that despite the risks, their service was a patriotic duty, a compelling moral obligation. "You have I know your share of patriotism," Georgian Clement A. Evans told his wife, Allie, "and you must not let your great love for me stand between you and your country." Strong Vincent, a successful lawyer in Erie, Pennsylvania, married his childhood sweetheart just before starting for the front. "If I live, we will rejoice over our country's success," he told his bride. "If I fall, remember you have given your husband a sacrifice to the most righteous cause that ever widowed a woman."

Hastily organized and led by officers who often knew nothing of military drill and regulations, the enthusiastic volunteers started for the front afraid that the fighting would be over before they arrived. At docksides and railroad stations across the North and South, the same emotional scene was enacted, as tearful families saw their soldiers off to war. "Some said goodbye carelessly," noted Lieutenant Abner R. Small of the 16th Maine, "fully believing that we should never leave the State. Others hung about the necks of loved ones, and only after embraces and kisses repeated over and over again, would they tear themselves away." Most troops traveled

by rail, and the journey in crowded boxcars often took on the air of a celebration. "All along the tracks of the railroad, men, women, and children, filling the windows of the houses and thronging the wayside, cheered us on our way," reported New York military surgeon George T. Stevens. "In the train, the men kept up a continuous cheering."

As they began their time in the field, most recruits were loath to dispense with all the comforts and luxuries they had known in civilian life. "The volunteer of 1861 was a very elaborate institution," recalled John S. Robson of the 52d Virginia; "the knapsack was a terror, loaded with thirty to fifty pounds of surplus baggage." Robson noted that many "high privates" in the Southern army had taken along "their own faithful body-servants" to see to the cooking and washing.

Even before the first tentative forays were made against their enemy, however, the troops mustering in the sprawling encampments of the gathering armies began to realize just how much they had yet to learn of the ways of soldiering. "Our first march made us realize that we must reduce ourselves to the lightest marching trim," Virginian Edgar Warfield remembered, "and the great cumbersome knapsack, heavily loaded with everything we thought a soldier might need, soon became a thing of the past." Sweltering in their woolen uniforms as they trudged down the dusty roads of Virginia or Tennessee, the soldiers cast aside all but the bare necessities, and the waysides were strewn with surplus clothing, shoes, blankets, and family keepsakes.

The first battles of the war made it clear to both sides that victory would never be won by troops whose enthusiasm failed to disguise the fact that they were little more than armed

Four pen-and-ink character studies by artist-correspondent Winslow Homer seem to confirm the observation of a Federal staff officer that some of the soldiers he saw were "slouchy, some dirty; but nearly all tough and strong looking." Homer traveled with the Army of the Potomac during the Peninsula campaign in 1862 as a correspondent for Harper's Weekly.

mobs. Accepting the grim realities of a protracted and costly struggle, the Union and Confederacy strengthened their forces with hundreds of new regiments and in most cases mandated at least a three-year term of enlistment. Discipline was tightened, punishment was meted out for even the most minor infractions of military decorum, and officers began to put their companies and regiments through a seemingly endless round of drill. As early as the second month of war, officers such as Major Wilder Dwight of the 2d Massachusetts recognized the need for military professionalism. "The voluntariness has died out in the volunteer," Dwight wrote. "He finds himself devoted to regular service. A regular he must be made, and the rules and articles of war, in all their arbitrary severity, will not sit lightly upon him."

Bridling at the new insistence on Regular Army notions of soldiering, an Irish-born private in the 57th New York grumbled to Corporal Cornelius Moore, "They give us *drill* for breakfast, *drill* for dinner, *drill* for supper, and *roll call* for sleep at night." Eighteen years old and full of fight when he enlisted, Corporal Moore was inclined to agree with his comrade. "It is enough to take the enthusiasm out of any young man," Moore wrote his sister, "to wait for two or three months cooped up in some small camp ground, fed on the coarsest of food, and drilled to death." Moore declared himself "sick and tired of the monotony of the life we are leading," and professed his impatience "to be about the business for which I left home and friends."

Many novice soldiers resented the necessary but nonetheless irksome imposition of a hierarchical military system. As Maine volunteer Abner Small expressed it, "we were machines to be perfected and used as

men like ourselves, holding commissions of authority, saw fit for the good of the service." Accustomed to the democratic freedoms of civilian life, the privates in the ranks often bridled at the tyrannical ways of their officers. Virginian Randolph A. Shotwell described "the bitter mortification of having to obey in silence the coarse commands of petty upstarts," who were "vulgar in speech, manner, and action, but clothed with 'a little brief authority' which gave them opportunity to domineer over men in every respect their superiors."

Eventually most men came to accept the disagreeable but inescapable realities of soldier life. "It takes a raw recruit some time to learn that he is not to think or suggest, but obey," Massachusetts volunteer Warren Lee Goss admitted; "I acquired it at last, in humility and mud, but it was tough." By the second year of service most regiments that had marched to war a thousand strong had been winnowed by battle and disease to less than half their original number. The men who remained were lean and tan; they were proud and resourceful, and they knew what was expected of them. They were, in short, veterans. "To look at our old men a year ago, and compare them with what they are now, the change is wonderful," wrote Major Henry Curran of the 146th New York; "they were mere babies then." As one Federal cavalryman put it, "Military life seemed to have become a second nature, a regular business."

A new recruit who joined the ranks of a veteran outfit would invariably be regaled with cries of "fresh fish!" and made the butt of good-natured but at times humiliating practical jokes until he was assimilated into the company. Newly arrived regiments, whose spotless uniforms and polished brass stood in stark contrast to the veterans' shab-

by, threadbare garb were dubbed "paper collar soldiers," and viewed with suspicion until they proved themselves in battle. Conscripts, draftees, and men who had been induced to enlist by the payment of a cash bounty were especially subject to ridicule and derision. When a woebegone group of conscripts arrived in the camp of the 4th Virginia, veteran Alexander T. "Ted" Barclay was moved to pity as he watched his comrades "whooping and making all sorts of fun over them."

Fighting for a common cause, facing a common trial, men of disparate backgrounds bonded in the ineffable brotherhood of arms. "The longer we associate together the more we become endeared to each other," Illinois soldier Thomas G. Odell explained in a letter to his wife, Beliscent; "necessity compels the soldier to make himself sociable and agreeable to his comrades." Virginia artilleryman Carlton McCarthy noted that "as time wore on, the various peculiarities and weaknesses of the men showed themselves, and each company, as a community, separated into distinct circles." Within those circles the men would mess together, share fatigue duty, and look after an ailing comrade. They had become pards.

The poet Walt Whitman, who had witnessed the suffering of war firsthand, found a spiritual vindication for the carnage in the indomitable nature of the fighting men. Not long after the conflict he wrote:

The actual soldier, North and South, with all his ways, his incredible dauntlessness, his superb strength and lawless gait, will never be written. No future age can know, but I well know, how this war resided in the unnamed, unknown rank and file, and the brunt of its labor of death was volunteered.

"I was full of the mental champagne that comes from a cheering multitude."

LIEUTENANT SAMUEL H. M. BYERS

5TH IOWA INFANTRY

Galvanized by the shelling of Fort Sumter, Northerners flocked to join the Federal colors during the first months of the war. Byers, then a 23-year-old lawyer, describes how he too caught the patriotic fever and ended up a soldier in a blue uniform. Captured at Missionary Ridge in the fall of 1863, Byers survived the horrors of a Confederate prison camp and lived into his nineties—long enough to see Franklin D. Roosevelt elected president.

It all came through a confusion of names. A patriotic mass meeting was held in the courthouse of the village. Everybody was there, and everybody was excited. A new regiment had been ordered by the governor, and no town was so quick in responding as the village where I lived. Drums were beating at the mass meeting, fifes screaming, people shouting. I sat beside a Mr. Myers, one of our prominent citizens. There was a little pause in the patriotic noise, and then someone called out, "Myers to the platform!" Mr. Myers never stirred. Again the voice shouted, "Myers! Myers!" Myers turned to me and said, "They are calling you, Byers," and fairly pushed me out into the aisle.

I was young . . . ambitious and now was all on fire with newly awakened patriotism. I went up to the platform and stood by the big drum. The American flag was hanging over my head. In a few minutes I was full of the mental champagne that comes from a cheering multitude. I was burning with excitement, with patriotism, pride and my enthusiasm lent power to the words I uttered. I don't know why or how, but I was moving my audience.

. . . In ten minutes one hundred youths and men, myself the first, had stepped up to the paper lying on the big drum and had put down our names for the war.

Members of the newly formed 1st Michigan Infantry receive the national colors before a throng of well-wishers in Detroit in May 1861—a time when fervid posters like the one at right (inset) were pulling in recruits from every town and hamlet across the land.

PRIVATE HENRY E. HANDERSON

9TH LOUISIANA INFANTRY

A native of Ohio and graduate of Hobart College, Handerson went to Louisiana in 1859 to work as private tutor to the children of a wealthy cotton planter. Later he was studying medicine in New Orleans when hostilities broke out. Handerson returned to the North after the war and enjoyed a long and distinguished career as a physician and medical historian.

Throughout the broad surface of the entire land the roll of the drum and the cheers of the gathering volunteers drowned all other sounds, and all business was paralyzed before the pressure of the impending struggle, whose desperateness and magnitude however, neither President nor peasant realized. About this period I joined a company of so-called "home-guards" forming in my neighborhood, and whose duty it was to maintain order among the Negroes and other suspicious characters of the vicinity. . . .

It seemed evident that a crisis had arrived in which it became necessary for every man to decide definitely upon his future course. Born and educated in the North, I did not share in any degree the fears of the Southerners over the election to the Presidency of Mr. Lincoln. I could not but think the action of the seceding States unwise and dangerous to their future prosperity. On the other hand, this action had already been taken, and without any prospect of its revocation. Indeed, in the present frame of mind of the North, any steps toward recession seemed likely to precipitate the very evils which the secession of the States had been designed to anticipate. I believed slavery a disadvantage to the South, but no *sin,* and, in any event, an institution for which the Southerners of the present day were not responsible. An inheritance from their forefathers, properly administered it was by no means an unmitigated evil, and it was one, moreover, in which the North but a few years before had shared. All my interests, present and future,

apparently lay in the South and with Southerners, and if the seceding States, in one of which I resided, chose deliberately to try the experiment of self-government, I felt quite willing to give them such aid as lay in my feeble power. When I add to this that I was 24 years of age, and naturally affected largely by the ideas, the enthusiasm and the excitement of my surroundings, it is easy to understand to what conclusions I was led. . . .

Thus it came about that on Monday, June 17th, 1861, I enrolled my name as a private in the "Stafford Guards," as the company of Captain Stafford was then called. . . .

The "Stafford Guards," as I have already mentioned, consisted largely of the sons of well-to-do planters, with whom were associated a few "roughs," chiefly denizens of the "piney-woods" regions north of Alexandria, and perhaps half-a-dozen Jews, most of whom had carried a pack along the Red River.

Leroy A. Stafford, a prominent Louisiana planter who organized Henry Handerson's regiment, opposed secession but became one of the South's fiercest defenders once the fighting began, rising from the rank of captain to brigadier general. Paralyzed by a bullet on May 5, 1864, the first day of the Battle of the Wilderness, Stafford died three days later in Richmond, Virginia.

PRIVATE ISAAC N. RAINEY
7TH TENNESSEE INFANTRY

One of 10 children, Rainey (shown at left in a postwar photograph) grew up on a small farm in central Tennessee. The company that he joined, made up largely of men from a prewar militia group known as the Memphis Light Dragoons, served as escort for the division commander, Brigadier General William Hicks Jackson.

Dressed in homespun and carrying weapons brought from home, the men of Company H, 3d Arkansas Infantry (above), muster in Arkadelphia, Arkansas, about 55 miles southwest of Little Rock, in June 1861. Two months later the regiment suffered heavy casualties at the Battle of Wilson's Creek in Missouri and was disbanded. The survivors were integrated into other Confederate units.

*I*n our community the boys were enlisting for the war; they were eager for war. They were full of enthusiastic patriotism. How few of them understood or appreciated why or what it was all about. I know that neither Joe nor I did, yet we enrolled our names on the roster of one of the three companies raised in Columbia on that day. Joe 17 the December before; I just 16. Pa having more sense than we, ordered our names erased from that roll. . . .

When President Lincoln called for 75 thousand soldiers to be used in the subduing of the South, Tennessee refused her quota. Then our people became more enthusiastic than ever. There were more volunteers, more companies formed. Joe and I became restless. We thought of slipping off with the first company that left Columbia.

One morning Pa called his boys around him. "Boys," he said, "We are going to have a war, a big one. It may last for years. I want you to take your part in it; and you shall when you are old enough. But I want you all to promise me not to go without my consent. Will you make me the promise? I dedicate my boys to the cause when they are needed and old enough." We of course promised him this.

A little later individuals began to appear in public wearing long knives made of horseshoe files, knives as long as their arms. They were very brave "with their mouths"; strutted around full of braggadocio—their cry "Just let 'em come; I can whip a dozen of the cowardly Yankees!" was the tenor of their cry. We noticed that none of these long knife braves volunteered. . . . Captain Taylor administered to me the oath of allegiance to the Confederate States of America and I became a soldier sixteen days before my 18th birthday. I weighed 111 pounds, was the youngest and smallest member of my company. How proud I was to be a soldier! To take a man's place in the great conflict! I resolved then that I would never do an act that my good father and mother would be ashamed of, that my own self-respect would not approve, that might besmirch our family name.

they reenlist for the war, but not many will be placed there as all seem determined to reenlist.

If we only can get out a big army in the spring, we can wind the thing up. Let the Volunteers reenlist and the cowardly Milish be drafted and placed behind breastworks if they can't do any better than they did at Bath.

Why must the thing be given up now? If it is not worth fighting for, it is not worth having. . . .

Good bye, Ted

LIEUTENANT ALEXANDER T. BARCLAY

4TH VIRGINIA INFANTRY

Barclay was a 17-year-old student at Washington College in Lexington, Virginia (now Washington and Lee University), when he joined the college militia company, the Liberty Hall Volunteers, which was mustered into the Confederate army in the spring of 1861 as part of the famed Stonewall Brigade. Despite his aversion for marching, Barclay reenlisted; in May 1864 he was captured at Spotsylvania and held in a Federal prison until July 1865.

February 10th
  Dear Sister, . . .
Everyone thinks here if the Volunteers reenlist we can put this war through in the spring. I never saw such enthusiasm; it beats the first of the war. Certainly everything is in favor of the South now. England and France are vying with each other who shall recognize us first. I think that they will undoubtedly do so before long.

I would reenlist but would have to go with the same service and as I do not like infantry I will wait until my term expires and go home and enter some other branch of the service. This thing of walking don't pay. I exclaim in the words of Richard, "A horse, a horse, my kingdom for a horse."

We boys are sweeping everything before us down here. The ladies don't stand a chance. I don't think Winchester will have any old maids left in it as everybody seems to have a Dulcenia Debosa.

I think every scoundrel in old Rockbridge who has been hiding himself in the Militia should be drafted. For are not the Volunteers fighting for their liberty while they are at home enjoying all the luxuries and we enjoying none? All are very much displeased at the bill passed by the Legislature placing the Volunteers on the draft with the Militia unless

CORPORAL JAMES GARVIN CRAWFORD

80TH ILLINOIS INFANTRY

Crawford's antipathy to the Confederacy, expressed here in a letter to his cousin, may have been kindled by a source close to home: His father participated in the underground railroad for escaped slaves in Illinois. Later in the war, however, after witnessing the wanton destruction of property by Union troops in the South, Crawford expressed sympathy for the Southern people if not for their cause.

Nashville, Tenn
Aug 4th 1863
Dear Cousin,

What do you think the prospects is for us staying our three years out. I think the prospects good for three year, and will be very thankfull if they have things all right by that time. For my part as far as I am concerned myself I would be quite willing to serve five years rather then see our good old government go down to such a depth of depravity as these infernal theifs and robbers of the south are trying to bring it to. If we were whiped and the Jeff Davis & Co. were to get the reins of government in there hands, do you think I would stay in these states—Never! I would rather live with the Indian in the forest and stand the hardships and privations that they are subject to then bow my knee to a traitor. I would rather live under the laws of Great Britain that our fathers threw [off] long ago. Yes, I would rather put my neck under the yoke of England then under the yoke of Tyrants and Traitors, but enough of this at the present time. . . .

    J. G. Crawford

PRIVATE ANTON SCHMIDT

68TH PENNSYLVANIA INFANTRY / 14TH CONNECTICUT INFANTRY

Schmidt had the misfortune to arrive in the United States from his native Germany in the spring of 1863, a time when war weariness had brought volunteering nearly to a halt and untutored young immigrants like himself were looked upon as potential cannon fodder. In this testimony written in 1909 to support his claim to a veteran's pension, Schmidt, who anglicized his name to Smith, describes how he was shanghaied into the army and wrongly accused of desertion.

I came to this country on May 10th, 1863, and proceeding from New York to New Haven, Conn., where I worked in a tin factory along with an old man, with whom I boarded. One day, about July 14th, 1863, this old man telling me to follow him, led me into a large building, (which I have since learned was an enlisting barracks) and talking to the man behind the iron grating, left me there saying he would return. I cannot say what he talked about, as I could not understand the English language. Directly two men came in and led me to another room, where my citizen's clothes were taken away and a soldier's uniform given me.

I was then told that I was enlisted under the name of Chas. Roehmer, and was at once forwarded to the front to Co. H, 14th Conn. Vol. Inftry. and was much surprised to hear them call me Roehmer, and of course did not answer at first until I was told that I must answer to that name. Well, I served in line of duty till I was wounded in the Battle of the Wilderness on May 6th, 1864, whereupon I was furloughed to Lincoln Hospital, Washington, D.C. for 30 days. A little later, while in New York City, I was again picked up and sent to a soldier's barracks at Jersey City, N.J. and notwithstanding the fact that the wounds in my right knee and left shoulder were still open, I was forwarded to the front, this time under my correct name of Anton Smith. When I arrived as far as City Point, Va., I was sent by a Dr. to Washington with a pass and being tired out fell asleep. Upon awakening I found myself 25 miles from New York City, and without a dollar in my pocket. I walked over to Hoboken, Union Hill, N.J., to a friend of my father's and asked for a loan of $50.00. He left through the back door telling his barkeeper to give me all I wished to drink, and soon reappeared with another man who arrested me and sent me to Trenton, N.J., from thence going to Alexandria, Va., where I was court-martialed and sentenced to forfeit $10.00 per month out of my monthly pay for 18 months for desertion from the service as Charles Roehmer. This was in October, 1864. In November 5th of the same year, I was forwarded to the Bull Pen near City Point, Va., when on Jan. 3rd, 1865, I was forwarded to Co. G, 68th Pa. Vol. Inftry. where I served in line of duty until June 9th, 1865, when I was honorably discharged as Anton Smith from this Regiment at Hart's Island, N.Y.

Coming from Germany as stated at the opening of this letter I was not acquainted either with the custom laws or languages of this country. I did not intend to desert and was in fact in the service continually, though knowing nothing of jumping bounties, I served with two companies. I have been wronged and taken advantage of, at every turn whilst in this country.

"Let us not talk of peace, if we must let the rebels come back with their institution of human slavery."

ENLISTING IRISH AND GERMAN EMIGRANTS ON THE BATTERY AT NEW YORK — SEE PAGE 285.

In this newspaper engraving newly arrived German and Irish immigrants in New York City listen to the pitches of Federal recruiting officers and private brokers beside a wall covered with bounty offers. Some largely German units, such as the 26th Wisconsin, advertised for recruits in German (inset).

*During lulls in the fighting a Union officer was often detailed
to return to his state to sign up new soldiers for his regiment.
He might take along a recruiting flag imprinted with the regiment's battles, such as this one from the 32d Indiana Infantry.*

PRIVATE ORSON YOUNG

96TH ILLINOIS INFANTRY

*Concerned that President Lincoln might be defeated by a peace-seeking rival,
Young wrote this letter to his parents in Lake County, Illinois, from newly
captured Atlanta on September 22, 1864, expressing his determination to press
on to final victory. Still a teenager, the writer himself was too young to vote.*

It is cowardly and insulting to the soldiers to talk of peace or cessa-
tion of hostilities after such a glorious campaign as ours has been.
Let us go on, till the rebels cry for peace and lay down their arms. Let
us not talk of peace, if we must let the rebels come back with their institution of human slavery. If peace could be had today with all things as
they were before the rebellion, I would not accept it. Slavery was the
cause of all this bloodshed, and it is madness to go back to slavery.

Four millions of human beings are suffering under the chain and the
lash. They have been appealing for years to the Almighty God for justice. In the anguish of their hearts, the slaves almost thought that there
was no God. But God heard their prayers. We are now paying the price
of our national sin. Shall we be so rash as to allow slavery to continue
and call the wrath of a just God upon us again?

Some men in the north are so afraid of having to come and fight that
they would accept peace on any terms. I have not suffered enough yet
to make me feel that way. Sometimes I have thought "what was the
use of it to me, if the union was saved and my life was lost?" Then my
conscience would ask me what I was born for—just to live for myself
alone? No I cannot believe that.

ATTENTION CONSCRIPTS!

HEADQUARTERS, 71st Regt. N. C. Militia,
Winston, N. C., February 6th, 1863.

I have just received an order from J. H. Anderson, Enrolling officer for the 6th Congressional District, and Dr. Edward Lea, P. A. C. S., Examining Surgeon, notifying all persons between 18 and 40 years old to appear at Winston on the 16th and 17th inst, for examination and enrollment. Particular attention is called to the following clause of the order aforesaid ;

"This notice includes every person between the ages specified—those who have been heretofore examined and discharged either by State or Confederate Surgeons—those who have at any time been discharged from the army—those who have furnished substitutes, and any and all persons who may claim exemption on any ground whatever. No person's discharge, exemption or detail, from any source, will excuse from attendance at the place appointed.

Attention is called to XIII paragraph, section 2 and 3, General Orders No 82, as follows :

2. All the laws and regulations applicable to deserters, shall be applied to such conscripts as fail to repair to the place of rendevous for enrolment or who shall desert after enrolment.

3. All the agencies employed for the apprehension and confinement of deserters, and transportation to the commands of their respective commanders, shall be applicable to persons liable to duty as conscripts who shall fail to repair to the place of rendevous after the publication of this call.

☞ Conscripts will come provided with at least three days' rations.

J. H. ANDERSON,
Enrolling Officer for 6th Congressional District.

Every free white male between 18 and 40 is required to attend, no exemption, detail or discharge, will release any one from attendance.

The commanding officer of each company in this Regt. will cause this order to be made known in every part of his District, and will also attend at the time and place above stated, with every free white male within his district between 18 and 40 years old.

By order of Col. J. MASTEN.
WM. A. CONRAD, *Adjt.*

Beginning in April 1862, when the Confederate Congress passed its first conscription act, Southern men were subject to draft laws that grew increasingly stringent as the war progressed. When North Carolina's Sixth Congressional District put out this registration notice, an eligible man could still gain an exemption by furnishing a substitute—a policy that was revoked in December 1863.

SERGEANT ROBERT D. JAMISON
45TH TENNESSEE INFANTRY

News of the fall of Vicksburg on July 4, 1863, and Robert E. Lee's retreat from Gettysburg the same day sent a wave of pessimism across the South. In this letter to his wife, Camilla, Jamison attempts to bolster her spirits by reaffirming his commitment to the fight. Jamison's unit was part of Johnston's Army of Tennessee, which surrendered to Sherman on April 26, 1865.

Tyner's Station, East Tennessee
July 28th, 1863 . . .
My dear darling wife,

. . . I am very sorry, dearest, to see you taking our reverses so much to heart and about to give the thing up because so much of Tennessee is invaded by the foe. Although many are in the same condition that you are—only much worse—still I keep in good spirits and am as confident of our success as I ever was in my life. Can see no chance in the world of our getting whipped if the people of the South will only hold out faithful and be true to themselves. Although many have become disheartened and deserted, I think there are enough left of the true steel to let the enemy know we are still in earnest and will never be their slaves. If our army is ever reduced so that we will not be able to procure our supplies and we have to disband our regular army (which I think will never be the case), we will then annoy them so that they cannot occupy our country in peace and will have to quit it because they can accomplish no good to themselves by trying to hold it. My opinion is that there will always be enough patriots left to poison the heels of all invaders of Southern soil. We are into this thing now and there is but one way to get out, and that is to stand every man firm to his post. The fact is that every man who had any soul at all would rather die than to be subject to the U.S. Government. I would, myself, rather fight the balance of my life and then be killed contending for liberty, than for you and our posterity to be under the rule of such a government. Life is sweet to me, but not so sweet that I would prefer slavery for me and mine to dying the death of a patriot. . . .

    Your husband with much love,

    R. D. Jamison

PRIVATE JOHN F. BROBST

25TH WISCONSIN INFANTRY

Private Brobst was recovering from minor surgery in the captured city of Atlanta when he wrote this letter to his future wife, Mary Englesby, then a 14-year-old girl. His anger at draft dodgers and Northern Democrats who favored a negotiated peace—the so-called Copperheads—was shared by most Union soldiers.

My headquarters in the hospital yet. . . . Sept. the 27th/64. . . .

We cannot hear anything about the draft, but the soldier's greatest hope is that old Uncle Abe will enforce the draft right up to the handle, and if he can't do it any other way, let about twenty thousand men go home and do it for him. We would like to go back and fight northern cowards and traitors than to fight rebels. They are the sole cause of myself and all other soldiers being in the field today. If they had held their tongues we would have all been at home now, but they must blow, and now some of them must fight at home or in the south. They will have their choice, and I hope if they do have to take soldiers home to enforce the draft that I will be one that will have to go, for I could shoot one of them copperheads with a good heart as I could shoot a wolf. I would shoot my father if he was one, but thank God he is not one of the miserablest of all God's creatures, a copperhead, a northern

OFFICERS OF THE 3D LOUISIANA NATIVE GUARD (CORPS D'AFRIQUE)

In April 1861 the state of Louisiana allowed black freedmen in New Orleans to organize a Native Guard under their own officers, but the guard was never called to duty. The following April, when Union troops occupied the city, the freedmen were mustered into the Union army by Major General Benjamin F. Butler, the military governor. Butler's successor, Major General Nathaniel P. Banks, renamed the guard the Corps d'Afrique. In May 1863 Banks heeded the petition below, sending the soldiers into action at Port Hudson, Louisiana, where they became the first black troops to fight in a major Civil War engagement.

New Orleans April 7th *1863*

    Sir we the undersigned in part resigned officers of the Third (3rd) regt La vol native guards and others desiring to assist in putting down this wicked rebelion. And in restoring peace to our once peaceful country. And wishing to share with you the dangers of the battle field and serve our country under you as our forefathers did under Jackson in eighteen hundred and fourteen and fifteen—On part of the ex officers we hereby volunteer our services to recruit A regiment of infantry for the United States army—The commanding Genl may think that we will have the same difficulties to surmount that we had before resigning. But sir give us A commander who will appreciate us as men and soldiers, And we will be willing to surmount all outer difficulties We hope allso if we are permitted to go into the service again we will be allowed to share the dangers of the battle field and not be Kept for men who will not fight If the world doubts our fighting give us A chance and we will show then what we can do—We transmit this for your perusal and await your just conclusion. And hope that you will grant our request.

"Send bog-trotters, if you please,
   for Paddy will fight—no one is braver."

LIEUTENANT COLONEL THEODORE LYMAN
STAFF, MAJOR GENERAL GEORGE G. MEADE

Scion of an old New England family and heir to an independent fortune, Lyman graduated from Harvard University in 1855. Shortly afterward, while on a scientific expedition in Key West with naturalist Louis Agassiz, Lyman became friends with Meade, who was at the time an engineering officer superintending the construction of lighthouses. In September 1863 Meade appointed Lyman to his staff. In a letter to his wife, Elizabeth, Lyman offers these opinions about the relative merits of Yankee and Rebel troops.

August 8, 1864

"What do you think of filling up with Germans?" you ask. Now, what do you think of a man who has the toothache—a werry, werry big molar!—and who has not the courage to march up and have it out, but tries to persuade himself that he can buy some patent pain-killer that will cure him; when, in his soul, he knows that tooth has to come out? This is what I think of our good people (honest, doubtless) who would burden us with these poor, poor nigs, and these nerveless, stupid Germans. As soldiers *in the field* the Germans are nearly useless; our experience is, they have no native courage to compare with Americans. Then they do not understand a word that is said to them—these new ones. So it has proved with the Massachusetts 20th (which has a perfection of discipline not at all the rule). Under the severe eyes of their officers the German recruits have done tolerably in simple line, mixed with the old men; but they produced confusion at the Wilderness, by their ignorance of the language; and, only the other day, Patten told me he could not do a thing with them on the skirmish line, because they could not understand. By the Lord! I wish these gentlemen who would overwhelm us with Germans, negroes, and the offscourings of great cities, could only see—only *see*—a Rebel regiment, in all their rags and squalor. If they had eyes they would know that these men are like wolf-hounds, and not to be beaten by turnspits. Look at our "Dutch" heavy artillery: we no more think of trusting them than so many babies. Send bog-trotters, if you please, for Paddy will fight—no one is braver.

At left, black and white soldiers gather outside a school built for the Corps d'Afrique at Port Hudson. By the end of the Civil War 300,000 black soldiers in 166 regiments had served in the Union army. Many of them learned to read and write in regimental schools like this one.

The Organized Bore

Writing to a friend 50 years after the surrender at Appomattox, Supreme Court Justice Oliver Wendell Holmes Jr.—a battle-scarred veteran of the 20th Massachusetts—recalled that "war, when you are at it, is horrible and dull." Holmes remembered that once during the conflict when he was at home recuperating from a wound, he was thought to be unpatriotic for remarking that "war was an organized bore." But half a century later, he wrote, "I am afraid my opinion has not changed."

Many old soldiers would undoubtedly have agreed with Justice Holmes. The typical Yank or Reb spent far more time battling boredom than he did the enemy. The monotonous drudgery of army life, with its ceaseless round of drills, guard duty, and fatigue details, tested the morale of even the most patriotic volunteers. Pennsylvania private Oliver W. Norton informed his family that soldiering was a "very slow business," in which "the stronger mental faculties are unused and of course they rust." Like all soldiers Private Norton welcomed the arrival of the regimental postmaster. "The boys laugh at me for writing so many letters," he noted, "but I think it as good a way of spending time as many others." Some of Norton's comrades preferred what he called "the spotted papers" —a deck of cards—to letter writing. "I don't know as I am principled against it so much," Norton wrote, "but I don't know how to play and don't care to learn."

In theory every regiment was supposed to have a chaplain, whose principal duty was to oversee the spiritual welfare of his military congregation—and in so doing bolster morale against the corroding effects of boredom and vice. Men of the cloth found their task a daunting one, and many resigned rather than continue their frustrating ministry. Samuel C. Baldridge described the challenge he faced when he reported as chaplain to the 11th Missouri: "Imagine me going into a gang of *rowdies*, vulgar, profane, gambling, shut off from . . . the influences of home & female society, without one solitary sermon for months & the

Federal soldiers take advantage of a brief lull in the fighting during the Wilderness campaign to bathe in Virginia's North Anna River below the ruined bridge of the Richmond, Fredericksburg, and Potomac Railroad. Photographer Timothy O'Sullivan exposed this plate during the last week of May 1864.

Devil having an unrestricted field in which to maneuver for their undoing & you may imagine the position I occupy."

For their part, soldiers were often scornful of clergymen whose stamina proved unequal to the demands of active campaigning. Union colonel Robert McAllister, a devout officer who saw that every man in his 11th New Jersey Infantry was issued a pocket Bible, complained that his chaplain preferred to ride in a wagon rather than march with the troops. "Chaplains ought to be where they can do good," McAllister wrote his wife; "he is of no earthly use to us here. He has not held a prayer meeting or done anything for the good of the regiment. He stays in his little tent and reads books, magazines, &c. He is disliked by us all. . . . He is a perfect drag."

Bypassing the hapless cleric, McAllister sought the assistance of the U.S. Christian Commission, one of several charitable organizations that had dispatched representatives to the forces in the field. The commissioners were more than glad to distribute their tracts to McAllister's soldiers, and much to his relief the colonel was soon able to report that 400 troops were regular attendees of the commission's evening prayer meetings. "Oh!" McAllister exulted, "what a blessed thing it is to have such meetings in the army!"

Occasionally waves of spiritual fervor would sweep through the ranks of an entire encampment, particularly during the long winter months of relative inactivity, when men had time to ponder their fate. "The whole camp was one religious gathering," David E. Johnston of the 7th Virginia wrote in the winter of 1862-1863; "there was a grand and glorious awakening." Confederate forces were particularly susceptible to religious revivals, with energetic ministers such as the Reverend Joseph C. Stiles, or Episcopal bishop-turned-general Leonidas Polk sometimes officiating at the mass baptism or conversion of hundreds of troops. "Until late hours, parties or congregations in many places may be heard singing and praising the great Jehovah," Alabamian Jasper James noted

in the spring of 1864; "may the work go on until we have an army fighting under the banner of the Cross of Christ as well as the dear Confederate flag."

In addition to fostering their soldiers' spiritual well-being, many officers encouraged a variety of sporting events as an antidote to boredom and a healthful alternative to the temptations of cards and alcohol. Holidays were frequently the occasion for inter-regimental competitions. The Army of the Potomac's Irish Brigade invariably celebrated Saint Patrick's Day with a steeplechase, foot and wheelbarrow races, climbing a greased pole, and what one officer described as "running after the soaped pig—to be the prize of the man who holds it." Baseball was an increasingly popular pastime, and in winter camp snowball fights would sometimes escalate to epic proportions. "It reminds one of a real battle," South Carolina soldier Taliaferro "Tally" Simpson reported. "To see a thousand or two men standing face to face throwing the white balls is truly exciting as well as amusing."

Another diversion for the soldiers was music, which was so prevalent that it seemed almost to provide a backdrop for daily life beyond the battlefield. "Musicians were a great feature of winter camp life," recalled

Guitars, such as the one at left used by a Confederate soldier, along with fiddles and banjos provided accompaniment to songfests and occasional dances in winter camps. Music was immensely popular in the ranks and was so important to Confederate cavalry commander James Ewell Brown "Jeb" Stuart that he arranged to have a celebrated banjo player, one Tom Sweeny, attached to his staff.

George Williams of the 146th New York; "violins, flutes, banjos, and the sonorous accordion were to be found in every regiment." Many units formed regimental glee clubs to entertain the troops, and amateur theatricals proved so popular that most winter encampments included several theaters, some capable of seating an entire brigade. Performances ran the gamut from Shakespearean dramas to uproarious burlesques, and for officers, the theaters also served as the setting for grand balls attended by visiting ladies. Lacking a female presence, enlisted men would sometimes hold stag dances, with soldiers dressed in women's attire.

Inevitably the time would come to sling knapsacks and shoulder muskets, as the armies prepared for battle. With mingled excitement and apprehension soldiers would abandon their camps and march off to resume the terrible business of war.

Members of a Federal army band prepare for a review at Fairfax Station, Virginia, in December of 1863. Trumpeter Henry P. Moyer of the 17th Pennsylvania Cavalry described his band as "a valuable adjunct to the regiment, especially for dress parade, guard mount, and reviews," and he believed it "accomplished much in relieving the monotony of camp life."

SERGEANT HENRY G. ORR
12TH TEXAS CAVALRY

Henry Orr and his cavalry company, the Ellis Rangers, reported to the camps around Houston, Texas, in November 1861. Stationed in the damp Gulf-coast lowlands in expectation of a Federal landing, the troop was overcome by sickness, a condition Orr ascribed to the climate and to "indiscretion" on the part of his fellow soldiers. As the men's health improved with the coming winter, they turned to sports and music to relieve the monotony of garrison duty.

Camp Parsons, Texas
December 21st, 1861. . . .
Within the last two weeks, the health has generally improved, and the boys are cheerful and gay. They have several ways of amusing themselves; the most popular one at present is town ball. Each company has some two or three Indian rubber balls, and they choose about ten or fifteen on each side. Such knocking, running, and shouting you never heard. The captains and lieutenants sometime take a hand. Lieut. Payne is hard to beat. They also play "Caste," "Cow Pen," running, jumping, etc. There is a string band in the regiment, and occasionally they have a serenade around the different companies and call out the Colonel and captains to make them a speech, which is generally responded to. They then have music and then call on the boys to sing jocular songs. Monsier Booker performs elegantly on his banjo, others on fiddles and the bass violin, and the time passes off very agreeably.

Federal heavy artillerymen, members of the garrison of Fort Greble, part of the Washington defenses on the east bank of the Potomac River opposite Alexandria, enjoy a game of baseball in the field near their barracks. The game was so popular in the Federal army that leagues were organized, complete with play-offs and championships.

LIEUTENANT ABNER R. SMALL
16TH MAINE INFANTRY

In mid-January 1863, Major General Ambrose E. Burnside, commander of the Army of the Potomac, ordered that Federal troops prepare to abandon their winter camps to go on campaign. In anticipation of long marches, instructions were issued to discard unnecessary gear. Abner Small observed his disappointed mates disposing of some of their favorite things, including carefully constructed game boards, furniture, and other such camp comforts.

M en are ordered to be in camp, and all surplus baggage and camp furniture disposed of, which means "destroyed for want of transportation." This includes all the handy things for housekeeping, constructed ingeniously from the bark and roots of trees. From bread boxes and barrels grew center tables, chairs, desks, and even cake trunks. Dice, chess-men and checker-boards abounded in every company, and to abandon all these was "cussid." One man in Company C dug a grave, and, piling in his little treasures, read service over them, and preached a sermon from the text, "And Ephraim fed upon the east wind three days and hungered not." A neat headboard marked the resting place of his jewels. On his return from the mud march, the grave was opened, and the numerous corpse resurrected without ceremony.

Two Yankee "pards" pose with their baseball gear in this wartime tin-type. The game as it was played during the Civil War used softer balls, such as the homemade examples at left, and the rules favored the batter, who could be put out only by a touch or by a thrown ball. A painted inscription on the bat identifies it as the property of Private George E. Tiffany of Company G, 15th Massachusetts Volunteers.

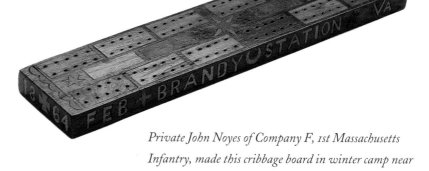

Private John Noyes of Company F, 1st Massachusetts Infantry, made this cribbage board in winter camp near Brandy Station, Virginia, in February 1864.

PRIVATE CHARLES F. MCKENNA

155TH PENNSYLVANIA INFANTRY

Boxing became a popular pastime in the 155th's camp near Warrenton, Virginia, during the winter of 1863-1864. McKenna, who had some experience in amateur boxing before the war, observed that the men in his regiment enjoyed it "heartily." McKenna joined his regiment shortly after it was organized at Pittsburgh in September 1862 and served to the end of the war.

Stripped to their shirt sleeves, with hats tossed into the "ring," two Federal soldiers square off for an impromptu bareknuckle boxing match in their winter quarters in an occupied Southern city. Enthusiasm for boxing grew with the arrival of prominent British professionals, who immigrated when their sport was outlawed in much of Great Britain shortly before the Civil War.

I have nearly finished a large drawing of this camp, which I have been working at spare moments the last week. It is executed entirely with the pen and will please you I think as soon as finished— We get plenty of exercise just now—Our company purchased a sett of boxing gloves some time ago—and few in the company ever saw or had such articles on before while I often used to practice with Irwin Street's best sparrers, and of course I learned some dodges then which give me an advantage over any I have yet tried them with—It is great fun for all—I have had them on a half dozen times; of course I shall not indulge in it to excess or get such a notion of my skill or sciences as to be ambitious to take every one in the regiment down—I tell you this confidentially—so don't let "Johnny Mackey"—P. R. or the editor of the *N. Y. Clipper* hear anything of this or I may spring into unpleasant notoriety.

LIEUTENANT CHESLEY A. MOSMAN
59TH ILLINOIS INFANTRY

Mosman, an Illinois-born mill-wright from Saint Louis, was promoted to lieutenant in 1863 for "meritorious service." Writing in his journal in 1864, he recalled the tribulations of a soldier in his company, Thomas Tobin, in learning to swim. The unfortunate Tobin was severely injured in a train derailment near Atlanta in 1864.

Tobin nearly drowned in the Mississippi at St. Louis Arsenal and I sat up all night with him after he was revived. He found he had gotten in over his head so he went to the bottom of the River and crawled nearly to shore when the boys saw him in the shallow water and got him out. Tom wouldn't give up his effort to learn to swim and whenever I went swimming—which was every time the opportunity was offered—Tobin went along. By the summer of 1862 Tom could swim a little and at Bowling Green, Kentucky, he tied a rope round his waist and giving me the end of it swam out into the stream. He got out well into the stream (half way across it) and turned round, started back. In going out he let the rope pass from his waist down between his legs and thence to me at the shore, and I stood on the shore holding it. He had thought the plan all out and wanted it done that way. In coming back the rope passed behind and over one of his legs and thence from him to me on shore. I did not know this and supposed the rope ran straight from me to his waist line. While swimming back his feet touched a rock that struck up in the bed of the stream and thinking to stand on it he let himself down but missed the rock and I, seeing him flounder, pulled on the rope. Of course, that pull made Tobin turn a somersault and he began to think he was gone, and his frantic efforts were no assistance to me in landing him. That experience was too much for Tom. He swore off swimming entirely and would scarcely use it for purpose of ablution. There is no fellow in camp that has contributed more to our amusement than Tom. It is too bad he got so broken up by the derailment of the cars.

CAPTAIN JOHN H. CHAMBERLAYNE
PURCELL (VIRGINIA) ARTILLERY

In October 1862, following the bloodbath at Antietam, the young lawyer turned artilleryman reported in a letter to his sister that he was "in a great rush of spirits generally & in exuberant health." In an October 20, 1862, letter, written while his division was halted for the night along the Baltimore & Ohio Railroad between Martinsburg and Harpers Ferry, Chamberlayne described an unplanned fox hunt through his bivouac.

Today somebody picked up a red fox, an old big fellow, in the grass, just as we got into camp near the Infantry. You see there were some 11000 or 12000 men camped around somewhat in a circle. The country was open, grass short, men eager as so many shouting school children; we had a glorious chase; the fox doubled & twisted, ran here & there, the men stumbled & fell about & yelled & pelted after him   All his doublings and turnings served but to increase his pursuers, so his thousand shifts led him but to his death. Some among the lousy crew, more fortunate than his fellows, caught him amidst such a hurly burly as you never saw. Verily, an army is such a monstrous sight that the very brute beasts stand aghast at it and their instinct fails at this unlooked for circumstance. Squirrels hares & partridges fall an easy prey & here an "old red" succumbed.

Soldiers often indulged in the favorite American pastime of whittling and found a supply of material in their cartridge boxes—soft lead bullets. Most bullet carvings, such as the ones above, were made for personal amusement and soon discarded.

CORPORAL JAMES GARVIN CRAWFORD

80TH ILLINOIS INFANTRY

In August 1862, James Crawford, a 19-year-old farmer from Randolph County, Illinois, enlisted in the service with the reluctant permission of his father. He was captured at Cedar Bluff, Alabama, on May 3, 1863, and paroled a week later. In a letter to his parents he described the hunger of his fellow soldiers for reading material and encouraged friends at home to mail good books and newspapers lest the men turn to dime novels and other less-enlightening fare.

Camp. . . .
        Blue Springs, Tenn.
        March 13th 1864
Dear Parents. . . .

   I received two "Tribunes" one "Free Nation" and some "Tracts" from you last night. Today having read the "Tract" I steped out on the alley or street in our Co. to give them to some of the boys, but hardly had got out of the tent till I was surrounded by the boys saying let me have one, and another would say let me have one. I gave them to two or three with instructions to read & distribute them. Reading matter is the call in camp and if friends do not answer that call by sending them good Books or useful papers, they will certainly be supplied with this worthless yellow Backed "Literature" so plentiful in every camp. I am certainly thankful that I have Parents that so well supply me with reading matter, while there is some even in our Co. that have never received a paper from home since they come in to the service. . . .

   James G. Crawford

Books such as The Soldier's Return (above), a pocket-size volume of verse published by the Pittsburgh Subsistence Committee, were sent to the regiments in the field to provide elevating reading material. This copy was owned by Private Seranton of the 186th Pennsylvania Volunteers. Most soldiers preferred popular novels of the day or dime novel adventures and romances. Newspapers and other periodicals were valued for their serialized fiction as well as their news content.

"During these days of wild soldiering the men were addicted to playing practical jokes upon each other."

PRIVATE SIDNEY M. DAVIS
6TH UNITED STATES CAVALRY

Sidney Davis, the 20-year-old son of a Pennsylvania farming family, left home to join the 6th U.S. Cavalry in July 1861. He served through Major General George B. McClellan's Peninsula campaign and fought at Brandy Station the following summer. He was captured by a Confederate cavalry detachment while on patrol near Emmitsburg, Maryland, in July 1863. Davis was held at Belle Isle prison camp near Richmond until September 1863, when he was paroled. He was discharged at the end of his term of enlistment, in July 1864.

Federal soldiers prepare to toss an unhappy "contraband," army jargon for a newly freed slave, in a blanket. A novelty to most soldiers from the North, blacks employed as camp servants were often the butt of cruel pranks and practical jokes.

During these days of wild soldiering the men were addicted to playing practical jokes upon each other. Sometimes when a party would be lying asleep around the campfire, with their boots out and their bare feet stretched out towards the welcome coals, a comrade would move a blazing branch closer to the glistening soles. Presently the sleeper would move uneasily and draw up his pedal extremities. Then the branch would be moved closer, followed by a similar movement, and this programme would be followed up until the sleeper had gradually travelled over considerable ground.

When at last the sleeper awakened, he would look about him with a bewildered stare, until the laughs of his comrades brought him to a realization of the pranks that had been played upon him.

There was another mode of dealing with soldiers accustomed to sleep with their mouths open. A long train of paper would be made and laid, with one end in his mouth, and the other off some distance. The end farthest away would then be lighted, and the paper would burn gradually up towards his face, and presently awaken him with its light and heat. On such occasions it was a comical sight to observe the curious emotions displayed upon his face—the uncertainty for a time, and then the sudden consciousness that brought him to his feet with startling suddenness.

LIEUTENANT JOHN V. HADLEY
7TH INDIANA INFANTRY

Twenty-two-year-old John Hadley of Hendricks County, Indiana, left North Western Christian University on September 13, 1861, to join the 7th Indiana. After recovering from a leg wound at Second Manassas, he was promoted to lieutenant. In the letter below, Hadley tells his fiancée of some entertainment at headquarters and assures her of his undying loyalty. Later wounded and captured during the Battle of the Wilderness, Hadley recuperated in a Rebel prison camp and made a successful escape in November 1864.

HQ. 2d Brig &c
Culpepper Va
Jan 31st/64. . . .

We gave an immense dinner party at our H.Q. last Friday. The day was set apart for a General Review of the Division & as many visitors were expected to be present at the Review it seemed good to the Gen to give all Officers a grand carnival at his H.Q. The day was as bright & fair as was ever known in Va & at 1 P.M. there might be seen youth, beauty, & chivalry assembling on the eminence that overlooked the plane where the Review would commence at 2 P.M. An immense crowd were present at 2 oclock when the troops marched on the ground. The Review was as fine as I ever saw for its size. Men looked well & moved by the Gen. with that stern look & sturdy step known only to battle tried veterans. After the Review 125 Officers repaired to our H.Q. . . .

We at present have two ladies on the Staff & are expecting *five* more from Baltimorr tomorrow. Also expecting to be reinforced in about a week with five more from Albany N.Y. making 12 in all. When they all arrive the women will be the controlling power of the H.Q. & what measures they will adopt for the prosecution of this war is very hard to conjecture. But I am not apprehensive that they will do anything unfavorable to "Union right or wrong." Surrounded by this multitude of uncompromising women I fear I shall be in mortal terror least I be forced into a policy of warfare very different from the one at present sustained.

But, darling have no fears. My heart is iron-clad & locked & there is but one key in the universe that can unlock it & that you hold. Keep it secure, dear, til God in His Goodness appoints a time for you to unlock it & take therefrom its jewel its all.

PRIVATE JOHN A. POTTER
101ST ILLINOIS INFANTRY

An immigrant from Yorkshire, England, Potter enlisted in the Federal army at Jacksonville, Illinois, in September 1862 and served throughout the war. He was captured by Confederate cavalry while guarding supplies at Holly Springs, Mississippi, in December 1862. Paroled by the Confederates, Potter was sent to Benton Barracks, Missouri, where he was exchanged. Writing after the war, Potter recalled a carefully planned practical joke played upon one of his messmates.

We had in our mess a man who went by the name of Bob who had an inordinate taste for sweet things. He never could get enough sugar. The army ration was entirely inadequate for his need, hence he was begging, buying or stealing it almost continually. In one of our camping places was found a variety of sand, a good facsimile of the sugar of those times. Jule, another messmate, brought a tin cup full of it and placed it on our humble board at dinner, all being in the secret except Bob, for whom it was designed. He poured out his coffee, and, with a large table spoon, he made a dive into the supposed sugar. One heaping spoonful was energetically stirred in, when he tasted, but it was not sweet. The second and third spoon, fuller than before, found their way into the smoking beverage, when, thinking it very strange it did not sweeten, he took a pinch, in thumb and finger, and inserted it in his opening maw, when he began to spit and sputter, to eject it from his mouth. Then Jule, in great indignation, remarked: "Bob, you great hog, I brought that sand up to scour my gun, and you have nearly wasted it all trying to sweeten your coffee with it." Bob innocently remarked he was very sorry; he thought it was sugar, when all the boys just roared with laughter.

"We had in our mess a man who went by the name of Bob who had an inordinate taste for sweet things."

Using swords, bottles, and fists, the officers of Major General Joseph Hooker's staff stage a mock brawl in their camp near Fairfax Court House, Virginia, in June 1863.

CORPORAL TALIAFERRO N. SIMPSON

3D SOUTH CAROLINA INFANTRY

"Tally" Simpson and his brother, Richard, sons of Congressman Richard F. Simpson, left college in April 1861 to rush to the defense of their state. Richard was discharged in 1862, ill with chronic dysentery, but Tally served in all of the major campaigns of the Army of Northern Virginia before his death at Chickamauga in September 1863. Encamped near Fredericksburg in February 1863, Tally wrote to his sister describing one of the exuberant snowball fights occasioned by a 10-inch snowfall.

Feb 27th

Dark came on too soon last evening and put an end to my writing, so I will endeavor to finish this morning. Every thing is quiet. No talk of a move, & no beef yet. The snow is almost gone, and our fun is at an end. Let me tell you what devilment we have been at. While the snow was plentiful, I, with the others of my mess and two more, thought we would have some fun. Having consulted, we determined to go in a crowd to the Col's quarters armed with eight or ten rounds of snow balls, put some red pepper pods down his chimney, throw a blanket over the top of the chimney, fill the tent with smoke, and then keep them in there with snow balls. We approached cautiously, covered the chimney, and then waited for it to take effect.

In the mean while, we had told Capt Langston, acting Lieut Col, of our plans and told him as soon as he saw the smoke begin to boil out from under the front of the fireplace to throw on more wood and come out and join us. He did as we directed, the fire blazed up, and the smoke rolled out into the tent in volumes. It soon got so thick that some one started out to examine the chimney to see what was the matter. No sooner than he got to the door than a dozen balls lit right on him, and then they began to smell a rat. They laughed, halloed, and begged us strenuously to have mercy on them. But twas no go. Finally they reached out their hands and pulled the canvas off. Capt Langston got me a saddle blanket, and I again covered the top, and this time held it on by main force.

The smoke by this time had become so thick & suffocating that it was intolerable—so much so that Maj Maffett cut a hole in the tent and stuck his nose through to get fresh air. Lieut Johnson, who happened to be in the tent, lay flat on the ground and poked his head under the door. They begged, threatened, and told us they would pay us back some day, all to no go. Finally they could bear it no longer, and they rushed out amid a storm of snow balls and lit in to fighting us like good fellows. But our party was too strong, and they had to knuck under. They enjoyed it as much as we did, and we all laughed heartily over it. I went to the tent and looked in, and the smoke was so thick that one could hardly see his hand before him.

After this scrape we went to Lieut Garlington's tent and liked to have smoked him and several others to death. They were afraid to come out, so they had to bear it as well as they could. The next night Lieut G and some seven others came round and blockaded our house. I happened to be on guard, and no one was here but Miller & Newman McDowell. The chimney was covered. The guard was stationed around the tent. The smoke soon bulged out. Newman saw it, smelt a rat, and broke through the back part of the tent and left old Miller to enjoy it by himself. McDowell soon came back with reinforcements and attacked the besiegers with spirit. Harry then rushed out, and they had a terrible combat. The whole company was against them, but it came out a drawn fight. The snow is gone, and the fun is up.

"AN EYE-WITNESS"
1st Pennsylvania Reserves

In a letter to the Lancaster, Pennsylvania, Daily Evening Press an anonymous soldier-correspondent recounted a hotly contested snowball battle fought by the brigades of Colonel William McCandless' division of the Federal V Corps. The action proceeded with proper military formations and tactics under the direction of the officers. The correspondent wrote from his camp near Bristoe Station, Virginia, in March 1864.

The day was beautiful, and the ground being covered with snow, it had such a dazzling effect, that the force was almost upon us before we could distinguish what or who they were. We saw them in the distance, advancing over the plain, their skirmishers in the advance, and their main force in the rear, but as they were inside of our lines, we could not think that they could pass our picket line without us knowing it, and had no idea that they were the enemy. . . .

. . . A skirmish line was advanced, and shots soon exchanged between them with a briskness that showed the eagerness with which the battle was accepted. Our men had long been wishing to have a tilt with the enemy at this place. The regiment being ready, it was advanced and they were driven across the railroad, but the track being high, the embankment afforded them protection, and conscious of their advantage, they defiantly and stubbornly held their position. At this point the shot flew thick and fast, and I saw a number of our brave fellows struck, and fall to the rear. At last, chagrined at the stubbornness of the foe, our men charged upon them in the face of a terrible fire and drove them from their cover, scattering them like chaff. They, however, received reinforcements from the woods beyond, where they had more troops stationed, and charging upon our men, they in turn had to fall back again to this side of the railroad. Our flag-bearer, undauntingly established himself on the track, and had with him some men and a supply of ammunition, when the enemy making a sudden dash, captured him and his colors, and with a triumphant shout rushed upon our troops and drove them back almost to the limits of our encampment.

CAPTAIN FRANCIS W. DAWSON
Staff, Major General James Longstreet

Englishman Francis Dawson arrived at Beaufort, North Carolina, on board the Confederate steamer Nashville as an ordinary seaman. He secured an appointment as a first lieutenant of artillery through the connections of Captain Robert B. Pegram, the Nashville's commanding officer, and soon after joined Longstreet's staff as ordnance officer.

The army was now into winter quarters, the men making themselves as comfortable as they could. Snow-balling was a favorite amusement, and was carried on in grand style, brigade challenging brigade to a sham fight. These contests were very exciting, and were the source of great amusement to the men. Practical jokes, too, were frequently played upon the officers. Mrs. Longstreet was staying at a house a mile or two from our head-quarters, and General Longstreet rode over there every evening, returning to camp in the morning. On his way he passed through the camp of the Texas Brigade of Hood's Division, and was frequently saluted with a shower of snow-balls. For sometime he took it with his usual imperturbability, but he grew tired of the one-sided play at last, and the next time that he was riding by the Texans, and found them drawn up on the side of the road, snow-balls in hand, he reined up his horse, and said to them very quietly: "Throw your snow-balls men, if you want to, as much as you please; but, if one of them touches me, not a man in this brigade shall have a furlough this winter. Remember that!" There was no more snow-balling for General Longstreet's benefit.

MAJOR FREDERICK L. HITCHCOCK

132D PENNSYLVANIA INFANTRY
During his regiment's brief nine months of service, Frederick Hitchcock fought in three bloody battles—Antietam, Fredericksburg, where he was wounded, and Chancellorsville. When his regiment was disbanded, Hitchcock was appointed lieutenant colonel of the 25th U.S. Colored Troops stationed at Pensacola Bay. Here Hitchcock recalls the festivities as the Irish Brigade celebrated Saint Patrick's Day in March 1863.

An interesting item in the experience that winter at Falmouth was the celebration of St. Patrick's day by the Irish Brigade and their multitude of friends. They were encamped about a mile to the south of our brigade upon a beautiful, broad, open plain between the surrounding hills, which gave them a superb parade and drill-ground. Upon this they had laid out a mile race track in excellent shape, and they had provided almost every conceivable sort of amusement that was possible to army life—matches in running, jumping, boxing, climbing the greased pole, sack races, etc. But the usual pig performance had to be omitted owing to the enforced absence of the pig. The appearance of a live porker would have stampeded the army in a wild chase for fresh meat.

The chief events were horse races. The army abounded in excellent thoroughbreds, private property of officers, and all were anxious to show the mettle of their steeds. Everybody was invited to be present and to take such part as he pleased in any of the events. It was a royal gala day to the army; from morning until night there were excitement and side-splitting amusement. Nor was there, throughout the whole day, a thing, not even a small fight, that I heard of, to mar the wholesome fun, until towards night our old enemy, John Barleycorn, managed to get in some of his work.

The chief event of the day and the wind-up was a hurdle and ditch race, open to officers only. Hurdles and ditches alternated the course at a distance of two hundred yards, except at the finish, where a hurdle and a ditch were together, the ditch behind the hurdle. Such a race was a hare-brained performance in the highest degree; but so was army life at its best, and this was not out of keeping with its surroundings. Excitement was what was wanted, and this was well calculated to produce it.

The hurdles were four and five feet high and did not prove serious obstacles to the jumpers, but the ditches, four and five feet wide and filled with water, proved a *bête noir* to most of the racers. Some twenty-five, all young staff-officers, started, but few got beyond the first ditch. Many horses that took the hurdle all right positively refused the ditch. Several officers were dumped at the first hurdle, and two were thrown squarely over their horses' heads into the first ditch, and were nice-looking specimens as they crawled out of that bath of muddy water.

In a sketch by Edwin Forbes, soldier-jockeys spur their mounts past the reviewing stand during Saint Patrick's Day races hosted near Falmouth, Virginia, by the Army of the Potomac's Irish Brigade. The March 1863 festival consisted mostly of horse races but included such diversions as sack races; contests of running, jumping, and boxing; and a greased-pole climb.

"Several officers were dumped at the first hurdle, and two were thrown squarely over their horses' heads into the first ditch, and were nice-looking specimens as they crawled out of that bath of muddy water."

"F. S. H."

On February 22, 1864, the II Corps of the Army of the Potomac held a grand ball near Brandy Station, Virginia, in honor of George Washington's birthday. A guest who identified herself only as F. S. H. was among a group of ladies invited by officers of the 1st Brigade, 3d Division, composed of men from Ohio and West Virginia. Of the ball, a correspondent for Leslie's Illustrated reported, "There were almost as many ladies present as gentlemen, and many of their toilets would have been worthy of notice in the most fashionable drawing-room of the metropolis of the nation."

How many soldiers who belonged to the Army of the Potomac, I wonder, remember the ball given by the officers of the Second Army Corps near Cole's Hill, three miles from Brandy Station, Va., on the 22d of February, 1864. . . .

Two hundred and ten ladies and comparatively few gentlemen not belonging to the army were present upon that occasion. We left Washington about 10 o'clock on the morning of the 22d, escorted by a committee sent up from "the front." We passed along through Catlett's, Bristoe and Rappahannock Stations, across Bull Run and the Rappahannock River, seeing rebel fortifications (then recently vacated), pontoon trains, block houses, and many places and things of which we had been reading daily, but never expected our mortal eyes to gaze upon. We reached Brandy Station about 3 o'clock and found numberless officers and ambulances waiting to convey us to our respective quarters. . . .

The quarters occupied by the Colonel of the 4th Ohio were given for the use of the ladies, and consisted of a log hut with canvas roof, and a wall tent back of it, the American Flag doing service as a portiere between the rooms. On one side of the front room was a fireplace, with a mantelshelf above it. A picture of the former Colonel of the regiment, Lorin Andrews, whose life as a soldier was so soon ended in death, hung in a rustic frame on the wall. A chandelier, prettily trimmed, hung in the center of the room. Two tables and some chairs constituted the remainder of the furniture. Beds came by magic, and only when needed. Time was too precious to spend much in sleep, as we had "enlisted" for only three days, and had much to do in that time.

As soon as we had shaken off the dust of travel we were invited to the chapel, which, for this occasion, had been converted into a dining-room, where we found, not bacon and beans, but a most appetizing dinner awaiting us. Everything, in and out of season, was before us, and after a blessing upon the food had been asked by the Chaplain, we lost no time in proving that we were capable of doing ample justice to the good things. Our long ride and fast inclined us, at first, to attend strictly to business, and not be particular about having our knives and forks keep perfect time with the music of the band, which was playing for our entertainment during the meal. But appetites were soon appeased and tongues loosened, and if there was not a "feast of reason," there was something much more common in those days, a "substitute" which answered as well.

The all-important ball was to come off that night, and we could not sit too long at dinner. Each lady was provided with an agreeable escort, and ambulances conveyed us to the headquarters of the 8th Ohio, where we disposed of our outside wraps before going to the pavilion, which had been erected for dancing and a supper-room.

The dancing-room, which would accommodate 25 sets at one time, was decorated with all the colors of the corps, and was lighted by 3,000 sperm candles, in chandeliers tastefully trimmed with evergreens. Artillery, small-arms, and pyramids of cannon-balls were placed in different parts of the room. The supper was all that could be desired, and it is not necessary to state that the music was exceedingly fine. The dancing was kept up till 4 o'clock in the morning without any Waterlooish interruptions, although we were near enough to see the flash of sunlight on the bayonets of "the enemy" the next morning. I have often wondered if that were not an item of information given to add interest to the occasion, and if those bayonets was not handled by some of Uncle Sam's boys. However, "I tell the tale as 'twas told to me."

We breakfasted at 9 o'clock, and were soon ready to attend a review of the Second Corps, which was to take place at Stephensburg, a place a few miles distant. Twenty thousand troops were reviewed by Gen. Meade, accompanied by his staff and a number of ladies on horseback. It was a grand sight to us who knew not then that it would be our good fortune to witness one superlatively grand "when this cruel war was over," and 200,000 troops should occupy two days in passing through Washington on their way home.

Upon our return from the review another good dinner awaited us, after which we went to see the 4th Ohio boys on dress parade, and to visit them in their barracks. We were invited to their "hall," which served as a school-room and for dancing. The sides were adorned with pictorial papers. The lights hung in the center of the room, and were trimmed with evergreens. From a beam which ran across the upper part of the room a large card was suspended, on one side of which was printed with pencil, "Lincoln, Seward, Chase, and the Union forever." On

Officers of the Army of the Potomac's II Corps and their guests spin beneath martial banners at a ball on George Washington's birthday in 1864. The vast plank-and-canvas hall was erected especially for the occasion.

the reverse side was, "Washington, Grant, Warren, Shields and Carroll." A table with schoolbooks on it stood in one corner. After we had thoroughly inspected the building we passed on to Co. H's quarters, where we found some of the boys singing. The place soon became so crowded that we were obliged to go outside, where we held an open-air concert. All joined in singing, "When Johnny Comes Marching Home Again," "Brave Boys are They," "Rally Round the Flag," and "John Brown's Body," with impromptu verses. By this time a fire had been made in "Amusement Hall," the ground floor had been sprinkled with sawdust, and an invitation sent for us to return and spend the evening there in dancing, which we were glad to do.

When we arrived a set was on the floor, made up entirely of gentlemen. Those representing ladies wore no hats, the others were excusable for keeping their hats on. Two flutes, two violins, and two guitars furnished the music. Our party again increasing in numbers, we went to the new brigade headquarters, not yet occupied as such, where we had three rooms. Dancing was kept up till nearly midnight, and a tempting lunch provided for us before retiring. We rose at reveille, and during breakfast, after much begging and pleading, we were furnished with our first glimpse of "hardtack." It did not, however, form part of the meal, but was converted into autograph albums, and the writer of this article knows of a piece which is still in existence. A fragment, too, of the 4th Ohio battleflag, which was considerate enough to be blown off while on review at that time, is a dearly-cherished memento of that interesting occasion.

But the time had come for us to be "mustered out." Our new-made friends and kind hosts went with us as far as Brandy Station, and the committee returned with us to Washington.

LIEUTENANT ALEXANDER T. BARCLAY

4TH VIRGINIA INFANTRY

After the Battle of Kernstown, Virginia, in March 1862, the 4th Virginia was moved up to Staunton. On duty there at brigade headquarters, Barclay wrote to his sister Hannah describing his pleasure in the music of the Stonewall Band. The band had been formed by eight members of the Mountain Saxhorn Band, who joined the 5th Virginia Volunteers in 1861 and were soon elevated to brigade status.

Dear Sister, . . .

I have just been listening to some of the most delightful music I ever heard. The band of the Stone Wall is out serenading tonight and came around and gave us a call. They played The Mocking Bird, Annie Laurie, etc., etc. It was truly a treat to hear them exactly twelve o'clock on one of the most beautiful nights. It really seemed that the moon had clothed itself in new garments and was endeavoring to rival in brightness its older brother the sun. Truly "Music hath charms to soothe the savage breast.". . .

The band has again struck up farther in the city. We are situated on a high hill which overlooks the whole town and can hear and see everything plainly. Everything is as quiet as can be. Ah, no. Mary Blair Jackson's brat has opened and is in full cry, not as sweet music as the band but quite as enlivening. . . .

Good bye, Ted

LIEUTENANT LOYD G. HARRIS

6TH WISCONSIN INFANTRY

Loyd Harris, a resident of Prairie du Chien, Wisconsin, was wounded at Gettysburg in early July 1863 while fighting with the 6th Wisconsin. Later that month he mustered out when his term of service expired. In an article written for the National Tribune in 1902, Harris praised military brass bands, stating that "no army in this or any other civilized country is complete without music."

At the commencement of the late civil war every regiment organized started to the front keeping step to the inspiring music of their own brass band, and while each and every one believed and was ready to take an oath that their band was the best in the army, our men were just as ready to wager anything from a box of cigars to a month's pay, rations included, that our band, that of the 6th Wis., was without exception, the worst of all.

On the march from Kalorama to the camp near Chain Bridge, an able-bodied private of Co. F broke his right leg in a vigorous effort to keep step with the dismal music from our band. It was a serious mistake when the higher powers allowed that band to go back "from whence they came." They should have been sent to the front to frighten the rebels with that one old tune—then followed by a charge by the entire brigade.

After a year in service, regimental bands were abolished, and only one allowed for each brigade. I remember how mortified we were once on a division review, where we were anxious to excel another regiment of our brigade. We had to march to the music of an Indiana band, a good one, by the way, but just as we wheeled into column of division and started to pass the General, with his staff, also a brilliant array of Washington belles and citizens, who were expecting a great deal from us, the band struck up an operatic selection, no doubt very elegant for a grand concert, but a flat failure for marching.

Our men lost step, and those in the front muttered subdued curses on the rear ranks, who were stepping on their heel, and trying to climb over their knapsacks, the line looked like a rail fence, and our mild and gentle Lieutenant Colonel, who was never known to have any vices or use an oath, lost his temper and was heard shouting, "Blank that blank band." They must have heard him, for suddenly the tune changed, the step was taken, and in perfect time the crack regiment of the division passed in review; yet how much easier it was for the old 2d with their band playing the only tune their Colonel allowed them to play, no matter how grand the review—"Rosy O' More." No opera for them.

"On the march from Kalorama to the camp near Chain Bridge, an able-bodied private of Co. F broke his right leg in a vigorous effort to keep step with the dismal music from our band."

Bandsman Samuel Prescott, of the 1st Massachusetts Heavy Artillery, gave his final wartime concert at Fort Warren in Boston Harbor on June 23, 1865. His handwritten music book includes such titles as "John Brown's Body," "The Pleasures of Solitude," and the "Tuloo Quickstep." The playbill at left was printed for a performance of "Il Recrutio," a comic opera performed in March 1863 by a troupe from the 44th Massachusetts Infantry while they were on occupation duty in New Bern, North Carolina.

Bandmaster Gustav Ingalls (left, at table), of the 3d New Hampshire Regimental Band, examines sheet music in company with the band's treasurer, Samuel F. Brown (center), and Deputy Bandmaster D. Arthur Brown in their encampment near Port Royal on Hilton Head Island, South Carolina, in 1862. Appointed post band for Port Royal, the 3d New Hampshire played music that, in the words of a veteran, "drew tears and cheers."

A spirited musical ensemble of Federal soldiers display their instruments—tambourine, banjo, guitar, violin, triangle, and bones. Such players helped while away hours in winter encampments and provided accompaniment for amateur theatrical performances and minstrel shows. Fragile wooden instruments were generally shipped back home before the campaigning season began.

PRIVATE JOHN D. BILLINGS
10TH BATTERY, MASSACHUSETTS LIGHT ARTILLERY

John Billings, a 20-year-old machinist from Canton, Massachusetts, served in the Federal army for three years and fought at the Wilderness, at Spotsylvania, and in the siege of Petersburg. Through it all, he managed to avoid sickness and suffered only one minor wound. In 1881 he wrote a well-received history of his regiment, and six years later he authored Hardtack and Coffee, a classic account of soldier life during the Civil War. Billings described his writings as "the pleasant labor of spare hours, with no claim for their literary excellence, but with the full assurance that they will partially meet a want hitherto unsupplied."

In some tents vocal or instrumental music was a feature of the evening. There was probably not a regiment in the service that did not boast at least one violinist, one banjoist, and a bone player in its ranks—not to mention other instruments generally found associated with these—and one or all of them could be heard in operation, either inside or in a company street, most any pleasant evening. However unskilful the artists, they were sure to be the centre of an interested audience. The usual medley of comic songs and negro melodies comprised the great part of the entertainment, and, if the space admitted, a jig or clog dance was stepped out on a hard-tack box or other crude platform. Sometimes a real negro was brought in to enliven the occasion by patting and dancing "Juba," or singing his quaint music. There was always plenty of them in or near camp ready to fill any gap, for they asked nothing better than to be with "Massa Linkum's Sojers." But the men played tricks of all descriptions on them, descending at times to most shameful abuse until someone interfered.

The fife and clarinet at right belonged to musician Lewis Crebe Everly of the 33d Virginia Infantry, part of the Stonewall Brigade. The fifes and drums of a regiment kept the cadence of a march and also transmitted commands to the troops in camp and in battle. Woodwind instruments such as Everly's boxwood clarinet were rare in Civil War-era military bands.

SERGEANT VALERIUS C. GILES
4TH TEXAS INFANTRY

Shortly after joining the 4th Texas in the spring of 1861, young Val Giles posed for this ambrotype at William Bridges' Picture Gallery in Austin. There, for one dollar, Giles purchased a silver star to pin up his hat to make himself look "more fierce and military." He served throughout the war, surviving a severe wound and imprisonment. Giles died in 1915 after a long postwar career as a state land agent. In his memoirs, Rags and Hope, he recalled the effect of an enthusiastic self-taught fiddler on his comrades.

Blank, a soldier in my regiment, had found an old fiddle in Fredericksburg after the battle, brought it to camp and paralyzed a whole battalion. He tried to smuggle his fiddle through and concealed it among the pots, kettles, and frying pans in one of the wagons. But as that poor old fiddle had but one friend in the regiment and five hundred enemies, it was discovered and reported. The owner was ordered to throw it away or carry it. He swore that he would not part with it, and carried it on his back.

During the long gloomy nights we spent in that old camp, he would sit for hours at a time and sing and saw, and saw and sing. He could neither sing nor play, but that was not for the lack of energy, perseverance, or practice. He simply had no music in him, and he was the only man in the regiment who did not know it.

His favorite songs were "Nellie Gray," "Kittie Wells," and "Lily Dale," three of the most plaintive old ballads ever written. He was the best-natured nuisance ever seen. We couldn't abate him. The boys would abuse him, reason with him, offer to buy his fiddle, pay him to quit, and threaten to smash the old fiddle into smithereens, but it did no good. The drawl and saw continued. In addition to the three songs I have mentioned here, he composed one of his own. It contained about forty verses and I am glad to say I have forgotten all but the first verse, which ran like this:

Ee way out in Texas,
A thousand miles from here,
I've got a little sweetheart,
Ee little mountain deer.
She's er settin' an' er singin'
An' er makin' Rebel clothes
While I'm er shootin' Yankees

Whar the Rappahannock flows.

Forty verses like that forty times every twenty-four hours, made up our ration of music. Finally a petition was drawn up asking the captain to suppress him, signed by every man in range of that old fiddle.

A committee was appointed and presented the petition. The captain was a good fellow, believed in individual rights, free speech, and free music. He declined to interfere, told the chairman of the committee that the nuisance drove him almost crazy at times, but Blank was a good soldier, homesick, and in love, so the noise was allowed to continue. That old violin followed us like an evil shadow. Blank was never sick, he was never absent, never missed a fight, and could always find some sutler to haul his "dear old fiddle" as he called it.

Great was the rejoicing in the Regiment when the news came that Blank's old nuisance had found a watery grave in the Rapidan River. The sutler who hauled Blank's fiddle was miles behind the Brigade, and when he came to the Rapidan where we had crossed the day before, he plunged in. Not being familiar with the ford, he drifted too far down stream, got into deep water, lost his goods, and would have drowned had it not been for some Georgia soldiers who were bathing in the river at the time. They saved him, but happily for us, not the fiddle.

"He could neither sing nor play, but that was not for the lack of energy, perseverance, or practice. He simply had no music in him, and he was the only man in the regiment who did not know it."

Men of the Essayons Dramatic Club pose near their winter camp at Brandy Station in spring 1864. When the soldiers of the Army of the Potomac's Engineer Battalion discovered that several of their number were musicians and others aspiring actors, they organized the theater company to alleviate boredom. The club took its name from the Corps of Engineers motto, French for "We'll try." Private Gilbert W. Thompson (page 50) sits in the middle row, fifth from right.

PRIVATE GILBERT W. THOMPSON

Engineer Battalion, Army of the Potomac

Gilbert Thompson, a gifted amateur artist, designed and produced sets for the Essayons Theater, a creation of the Engineer Battalion, in their camp near Ashleigh Plantation at Brandy Station, Virginia. With the blessings of the unit's commander, Captain George H. Mendell, the engineers erected the theater with carefully trimmed pine logs. Private Thompson, in addition to designing scenery, kept a sketchbook to record his wartime experiences.

February 21, 1864. Pleasant; inspection; Sunday Service. All so-so. Since last date, one evening in our theatre, a Mr. Rockwell lectured on "Here and There in Europe," it was quite good, but the best of all was that it seemed like times at home, and [we] really felt quite a self-gratification, it was our work and something that is a credit to the battal'n. the stage appeared quite neatly and pretty, my landscape scene standing out finely,—stage scenery is very simple, if one knows how. The boys are rehearsing Toodles, which will go pretty well I guess. It made me think of old times. The evening of the 22nd. We had an impromptu "gander dance" at the theatre. I acted as sort of manager. We had cotillions, shottisches, polkas, waltzes. It was a success, all having a grand good time Capt. Mendell kindly postponing tattoo, no salutes were heard. The theatre is now completed and tomorrow evening, Toodles will be produced. I am only scenic artist, my violincello not yet arriving; a number of musicians are expected from elsewhere.

Private Edward Coolidge (above, left) and drummer William Clarke, two members of the Engineer Battalion, pose in character for a play performed in the Essayons Theater. The engineers put on plays with such titles as Toodles, Box and Cox, and William Tell. Performances of The Limerick Boy and Irish Assurance earned the theater $46 at 26¢ per ticket.

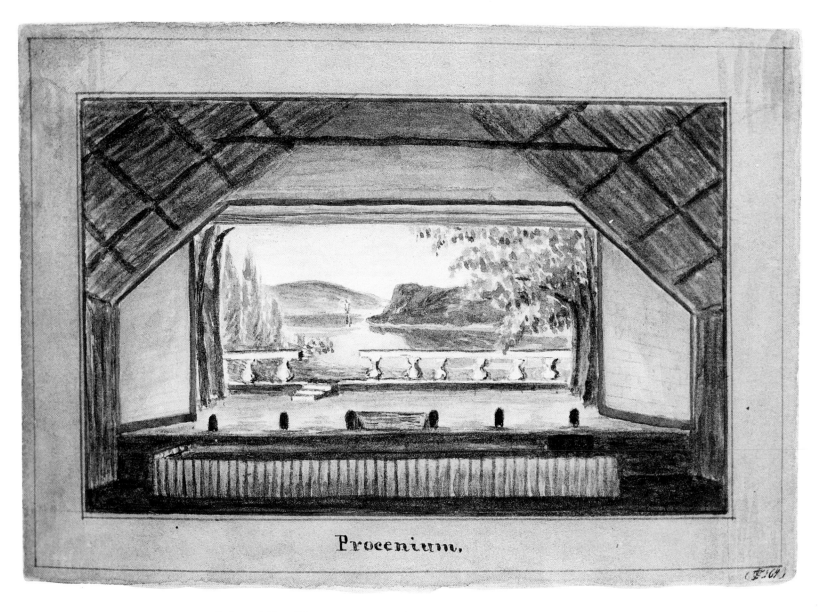

Procenium.

Private Gilbert Thompson prepared this watercolor design of a backdrop for a play performed at the Essayons Theater in the winter of 1864. The Engineer Battalion's theatrical activities came to an abrupt end in April, when a refusal to admit enlisted men to a production prompted a brawl. "The theatre is lonely and gutted now," lamented Private Thompson, "no more will ladies night grace its boards, or heroes of the dramatist stalk and swagger out their little hour of much greatness, no longer will be heard the sweet strains of musical violin and flute."

LIEUTENANT COLONEL WILLIAM W. BLACKFORD

STAFF, MAJOR GENERAL J. E. B. STUART

After Antietam in September 1862, Stuart and his staff spent the winter at the Bower, the gracious home of Stephen Dandridge near Martinsburg, Virginia. There, Blackford recalled, officers entertained themselves with rounds of playacting and games, much of which were instigated by the cosmopolitan Prussian Heros von Borcke.

Our General was the life of the party but he was ably seconded by von Borcke, Pelham and others of his staff, together with officers of cavalry regiments encamped near by, among whom was Colonel Brien of the 1st Virginia. Von Borcke was a thoroughly accomplished man of the world, and having been an officer of a household regiment in Berlin, in such a position he had acquired great facility in contributing to the pleasure of others in society. . . . Private theatricals, tableaux and many games new to us, von Borcke introduced.

One amusing series of scenes these two figured in which I had never seen before. A sheet was stretched across the hall, against which from behind the shadows of the actors were cast. The range of subjects adapted to this style is limited, but within its scope when well executed the effect is capital. A scene in which von Borcke lay stretched on a couch with Mr. Dandridge's capacious nightshirt on, stuffed to enormous size with pillows, was very amusing. The scene opens by roaring groans from this huge sick man, nurse appears and is sent for the doctor. The doctor, Colonel Brien, in an old mashed stovepipe hat, huge spectacles, an old-fashioned swallow-tailed coat of some Dandridge of past generations, and a bottle of physic with a streaming label attached to the neck, appears, or at least his shadow appears, and in a voice perfectly disguised begins his professional jargon with the patient. A deep draught from the bottle is administered to the sick man, and then, on

the sly, the doctor takes one too, to the great delight of the audience. Between groans and ludicrous twitches of agony the sufferer communicates to the doctor that he has been to a dinner party and enumerates a long list of articles upon the bill of fare which he had consumed, comprising beef, venison, oysters, cabbage, etc. The doctor pulls up the corners of his huge standing collar, protruding away beyond his chin, lays down the old battered fragment of an umbrella tucked under his arm, and proceeds to feel the pulse and examine the tongue, pressing his hand from time to time upon the mountain of a stomach beside him, at which the patient screams and writhes and says, "Mein Gott! Mein Gott! Doctor!" Having informed the sick man in a ludicrous professional manner what is the matter, the doctor proceeds to relieve the patient by forcing his arm down his throat and, with great effort of muscular power expended in jerks and tugs, pulls out in succession, and holds up for inspection, a pair of deer's horns, some beef's horns, cabbages, stalks and all, quantities of oyster shells, etc., etc., and finally a pair of boots. At each delivery an assistant concealed behind the couch abstracts a pillow from under the nightshirt, and expressions of relief follow from the patient until a complete cure is effected and the reduced man springs up, embraces the doctor and they begin swigging at the bottle of physic with the long label attached, until they become tipsy, and the performance closes in an uproarious dance of doctor and patient. The effect of forcing the arm down the throat was, of course, produced in shadow by running the arm down alongside of the face. The wit and humor displayed in this performance I have rarely seen equalled and its effect on the audience was convulsive. All the negroes on the place were allowed to come in to see it and their intense appreciation of the scene, and their rich, broad peels of laughter added no little to its attractions.

One evening, when there was an invited company and the parlors were all full, von Borcke and Brien gave us another capital performance. They were to appear as Paddy and his sweetheart. Mr. and Mrs. Dandridge were the only two persons in the secret, and von Borcke and Brien were taken upstairs secretly for preparation under their care. Von Borcke was transformed into a blushing maiden weighing two hundred and fifty pounds and six feet two and a half inches tall; a riding skirt of one of the girls, supplemented by numerous dainty underskirts and extended by enormous hoops according to the fashion then in vogue, hung in graceful folds to conceal the huge cavalry boots the huge damsel wore. Her naturally ample bosom palpitated under skillfully arranged pillows, and was gorgeously decorated with the Dandridge fam-

Major Heros von Borcke, a former Prussian dragoon, joined General Jeb Stuart's staff in June 1862 as an aide-de-camp. The six-foot-four, 240-pound officer was an imposing presence and an engaging and entertaining companion for his fellows at headquarters. Major von Borcke was severely wounded in the throat at Middleburg, Virginia, in June 1863. He left the Confederate service and returned to Europe the following year.

"A deep draught from the bottle is administered to the sick man, and then, on the sly, the doctor takes one too, to the great delight of the audience."

ily jewelry and ribbons, while "a love of a bonnet," long braids of hair, and quantities of powder and rouge completed her toilet, and in her hand she flirted coquettishly a fan of huge dimensions. Colonel Brien was admirably disguised as an Irishman dressed in holiday clothes, with a flaming red nose, Billycock hat, a short pipe, and a short, thick stick stuck under his arm. The absence of these two had been accounted for on some plausible pretext, so that when they made their appearance in the ballroom the surprise was complete. Both acted their parts to perfection. Paddy entertained the fair girl on his arm with loud and humorous remarks as they sauntered around the room, to which she replied with a simpering affectation that was irresistably ludicrous. No one had the faintest conception as to who they were, so perfect was the disguise. Before the company recovered from the surprise of their appearance the music struck up a lively waltz, and round and round the couple went, faster and faster went the music, and faster and faster flew the strangers. It was not until in the fury of the whirling dance, with hoop skirts flying horizontally, that twinkling amid the white drapery beneath, the well-known boots of von Borcke betrayed the first suspicion of who the lady was. As suddenly as they had come they vanished, waltzing out through the open door and followed by convulsive roars of laughter from the delighted audience.

A Question of Character

Writing home to his brother early in 1863, Private Edward K. Wightman of the 9th New York Volunteer Infantry had nothing complimentary to say about his fellow enlistees. He allowed that no sensible man would choose—perhaps "endure" would be a better word—the company of these characters who had been thrown together in the new regiment in the name of defending the republic.

"As a mass," Wightman noted, "they are ignorant, envious, mercenary, and disgustingly immoral and profane . . . almost every one drinks to excess when the opportunity offers, chews and smokes incessantly, and swears habitually." As the college-educated son of a prominent Manhattan attorney, Wightman was not the typical Yankee private. But while his scornful comments smack somewhat of snobbery, his assessment of the coarsening effect of military life on man's better nature rang with truth; indeed, it was an inescapable reality of soldiering.

It fell to the officers of a regiment, many of whom were green in military matters themselves, to mold their free-spirited and occasionally unruly subordinates into a disciplined fighting machine. In an effort to maintain control, many officers assumed a distant and formal authoritarianism that only earned the ire and enduring enmity of the men in the ranks. Soon after his return to civilian life following two years of service as a private in the 5th New York Zouaves, Alfred Davenport recorded a list of nicknames he and his comrades had assigned to their regimental officers. One captain with a penchant for meting out punishments was "The Fiend," a particularly stubborn adjutant "Bull Head," a corpulent lieutenant "Fatty," and Regimental Surgeon James Doolittle "Do-Less." In noting that Major George Duryea's nickname among the ranks was "Shell-fever," Davenport described the field officer's career as "one long record of meanness, domineering persecution, and cowardice." This much-despised major, the private declared, "is unfit to be called a human being."

Surrounded by an array of musical instruments, Surgeon David MacKay of the 29th U.S. Colored Infantry (second from right) enjoys a game of cards with fellow officers in his quarters near Petersburg, Virginia, in 1864. Open bottles of liquor and well-filled tumblers add to the conviviality of the occasion.

However he was regarded by the troops, an officer faced a constant battle to maintain discipline in the ranks, for soldiers pursued various unmilitary habits with relentless enthusiasm. Gambling was endemic in the ranks of both armies. Games of chance such as poker, chuck-a-luck, and old sledge were played in marathon sessions, often orchestrated by professional gamblers and cardsharps. Those officers who considered gambling a moral evil—or at least subversive of military routine—periodically tried to suppress the card games, but to little avail. "The gamblers hid in the depths of the forest," noted South Carolinian Berry Benson. "One part of the forest was dubbed 'chuck-a-luck woods.'"

"The gambler never lacked clients," observed Valerius Giles of the 4th Texas. "He carried his greasy old deck of cards with him and caught suckers wherever he went." Giles watched soldiers "who never threw a card before the war began. . . . lose the last Confederate dollar they had, betting at a game they really knew nothing about."

Nothing proved more disruptive to the enforcement of military discipline than that timeless bane of the soldier—liquor. The mid-19th century was a hard-drinking era in general, but particularly in the military. Although theoretically restricted for the use of senior officers, kegs of "commissary whiskey" were a common sight in army camps. The prevalent use of spirits for "medicinal" purposes meant that most regimental surgeons had a stock of "commissary" on hand, and bottles of patent medicine—most with a high alcohol content—were widely available.

Many volunteers who had been moderate drinkers before the war gave way to temptation as a means of escaping the boredom of soldier life. Louisianan William Watson observed that "men who had always before been strictly sober in their habits were now to be seen reeling mad with drink." Writing home from Memphis, Tennessee, in May of 1863, Ohio private George Cadman remarked, "Women and whiskey are plentiful

Playing cards manufactured by Goodall & Sons, a London firm, sport a motif of Southern naval flags surmounting the Great Seal of the Confederacy. Run through the Federal naval blockade, imported cards such as these would have been an expensive luxury in the wartime South. Men in the ranks, smitten by the passion for gambling that occasionally swept the armies, probably made do with cheaper or homemade versions.

here, and the men had been so long debarred from both that it did not take them long to raise hell generally. . . . the camp was a wild scene of debauchery."

Efforts by commanding officers to enforce prohibition were invariably thwarted by the cleverness of their troops. When Confederate general Thomas J. "Stonewall" Jackson ordered dozens of whiskey barrels staved in and their contents poured into the Potomac River, a group of thirsty Rebels just downstream retrieved the diluted but nonetheless potent residue by means of buckets tied to the end of ropes. During a railroad stop en route to the front, a group of 1st Arkansas troops wandered into town, purchased a coffin from a local undertaker, and filled it with jugs of "red eye." Then, as Private William E. Bevens recalled, "with sad faces and measured steps they carried it solemnly to the train." One Federal soldier convinced a local woman who had permission to sell pies and cakes in camp to tie bottles of liquor to the hoops beneath her dress. A sentry figured out the ruse when he heard "an audible jingle" but allowed her to pass because "it was such a clever trick that it deserved success."

Mischievous exploits like these served to bond comrades in arms even as they tested the limits of their officers. But in every outfit there were men set apart by their unpopularity, and Civil War soldiers developed their own terminology for those who failed to fit in.

A man who was perpetually awkward at drill, or whose clumsiness would inevitably upset the coffeepot whenever he came near a campfire, was termed a jonah. Chronic complainers were called grunters—they "complain, growl, grumble and brag," Pennsylvania captain David Acheson noted, "and yet are worth nothing except for stopping bullets." A soldier who avoided work details was known as a beat, and habitual shirkers as deadbeats, while officers who preferred rear-echelon assignments to combat duty were called coffeecoolers. John C. Lang of the 100th Illinois believed that many of these men were in fact "constitutional cowards," who generally managed to be absent from their units when battle was imminent. "It was some time before you could realize that the most dangerous weapon such a soldier ever shot off was his mouth," Lang concluded.

In a war in which disease claimed more lives than bullets, a favorite ploy of those who sought to escape drill or fatigue duty was to feign illness at the daily sick call, in which ailing enlisted men presented themselves to the regimental surgeon for examination. Some men proved remarkably adept at "playing old soldier," as the practice was known. Major Silas Grisamore of the 18th Louisiana recalled one Confederate who appeared to have suffered a stroke, "hobbling around on crutches with leg and arm shaking about." The man fooled everyone

who saw him, including the medical personnel, and was given a disability discharge. Grisamore noted that another fraudulent patient took so much medicine and "went through all the maneuvers of a sick man so completely that his deception became a reality. . . . depositing him in the cemetery."

In his classic study of the Civil War military experience, *Hardtack and Coffee,* Massachusetts artilleryman John Billings stated that "if a man was a shirk, or a thief, or a beat or a coward or a worthless scoundrel generally in the army, it was because he had been educated to it before he enlisted." But whatever their peacetime characters may have been, malingerers were to be found in the ranks of even the best-disciplined units. New Yorker Edward Wightman thought that most regiments were fairly evenly divided between conscientious soldiers—or duty men—and beats.

In fact, many duty men appreciated the rigid structure of military service as having turned their previously aimless lives in a positive direction. Irish immigrant Peter Welsh, who overcame his prewar bouts with alcoholism and earned promotion to color sergeant of the 28th Massachusetts, was contemptuous of those who bridled against authority. "If it were not for the discipline," Welsh wrote, "more than half of them would die for want of exercise. . . . plenty of exercise is the best medicine in the army."

PRIVATE RANDOLPH A. SHOTWELL

8TH VIRGINIA INFANTRY

In August 1861 at the age of 16, Shotwell (shown here in a postwar photograph), the son of a Virginia preacher, left prep school in Pennsylvania, sneaked through the Federal lines, and enlisted in the first Confederate regiment he found—the 8th Virginia. In this selection from his memoirs, he recalls his first night in camp.

The captain peered into tent after tent seeking a vacant corner to "stow away" the new recruit, but at each was greeted by a chorus of exclamations that there was not an inch of room; that the occupants were already "thick as fleas"! At length, at the last tent, the very bottom of the row in more than one respect, he bade me enter. "Crowd up, men, crowd up!"—he cried—"make room for this new man." There were seven large men rustling amid the straw and swearing they were already packed one on top of another. "Can't help it"—said he—"you must squeeze in somehow." This last remark was addressed to me. Then he walked off to have a smoke with the colonel, leaving me to find a bed if I could.

It was too dark to distinguish faces, but the spectacle of seven men prone in the straw was so much like a pig-pen that I laughed outright, whereupon one of them recognized me, and amid much cursing of the officers made room for me "spoon-fashion." However, I soon crawled out to sit in the doorway. The night was very hot and sultry—precursor of a thunder-storm, and the odor of seven pairs of unwashed feet filled the interior of the tent with nauseating oppressiveness.

Right here let me suggest that perhaps few readers appreciate the difference,—the disproportion, in the sacrifices of different persons, and classes in our calamitous struggle for Southern freedom. Differences in health, in wealth, in temperament, in culture, in social rela-

tions, and in domestic circumstances were so great that there could be no sort of comparison between the patriotism of different members of the same company, from the same county, or even family.

Take, for example, a wild rollicking youngster, without family ties, fond of outdoor life, and male companionship, careless of books or newspapers, and easily amused by a game of cards, "a fight or a footrace," who would therefore rather volunteer than to stay at home and work in the shop or on the farm. What equality of sacrifice was there in his case as compared with another young man of the same age, with a wife and children needing his care, or an aged mother, begging him to stay; with no predilections for a hardy life, but with a thousand reasons for pursuing other plans, yet who drops all personal considerations, leaves his family to the charity of outsiders, and goes forth to obey the call of his State! Or how shall we adjust the difference between the strong healthy man who, after marching all day, slept like a log, while his weakly comrade staggered wearily into camp three hours behind the rest and sat all night propped against a tree, barking with a consumptive cough! Both may have been patriotic, but surely not equal in self-sacrifice.

Camp-life to one may not always have been *pleasant;* but to the other it was *continual misery.* Some men suffered from *deprivations,* such as books, letters, and intellectual food, which were never once thought of by the majority of their comrades.

Some men were accustomed to rough ways of living before they volunteered in the army; whereas, for my part I can truthfully say I suffered more from coarse dirty food, dirty blankets and clothes; unwashed linen, (often marching and fighting for weeks without opportunity to wash our faces once a day,) and the ineradicable camp-vermin, than from all other hardships of the service. Perhaps I ought to include the bitter mortification of having to obey in silence the coarse commands of petty upstarts from corporals to captains and colonels, vulgar in speech, manner, and action, but clothed with "a little brief authority" which gave them opportunity to domineer over men in every respect their superiors. In recalling my four years of military service, these features of personal discomfort from lack of proper outfit, annoyance from rough and uncongenial associates, and sore humiliation under official arrogance far exceed the mere physical hardships and sufferings.

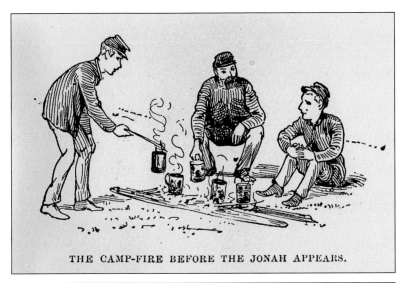

THE CAMP-FIRE BEFORE THE JONAH APPEARS.

THE CAMP-FIRE AFTER THE JONAH APPEARS.

A jonah—the kind of hapless blunderer found in every company—enrages his messmates by stumbling on the rails supporting their pots of brewing coffee, dousing their campfire, and wasting their precious rations. These illustrations by Charles Reed are from John D. Billings' Hardtack and Coffee, one of the classic accounts of Civil War soldier life, published in 1887. Both Billings and Reed served in Massachusetts light artillery regiments in the Army of the Potomac.

SERGEANT GEORGE H. WORDEN
16TH NEW YORK HEAVY ARTILLERY

Sergeant Worden wrote this reminiscence of the "galoot," or jonah, in his regiment, a soldier named Hake, for the March 28, 1895, edition of the National Tribune, the official newspaper for Union veterans. Hake later redeemed himself in the eyes of his comrades by heroically saving the regiment's colors during a Confederate counterattack at Deep Bottom Run, Virginia, during the Petersburg campaign in late July 1864.

Who that ever entered the service of our Uncle Sam does not remember the army galoot? He was on the right or on the left, in the front or rear rank, but always there, even in the crack regiment of each State. His clothes gave him away at the first glance. His cap was stuck on the back of his head, with top pushed heavenward; his pants and dress coat never matched for size and seldom fitted. If the coat was large the pants would be too small, or vice versa. Sometimes he would hop-skip into step, but more often he would only succeed in doing so after he had deranged the step of all the men in his rear.

He was also prone to step on his file-leader's heels, or, if carrying his gun at a right-shoulder, to prick the eyes out of the fellow in his rear. He always forgot half his duffel, and wanted to go back after he had been on a march an hour or more. He never could order arms without knocking off all the toes of the man on his right.

The other fellows always stole his blankets and defaulted on the tobacco they borrowed of him; ditto postage stamps. Generally speaking, he was always out of luck, and pretty often homesick and lousy.

Our regiment had a shining example of this kind. He probably received more damning the first six months after his enlistment than any President who ever vetoed pension bills. Poor devil, how I used to pity him. The officers had to take him out of the ranks and put him in the cook-house, for fear of mutiny. There it was worse, for he hadn't been there two days before he put sugar in the bean-soup and salt in the coffee. Then he upset the camp-kettle on the Commissary-Sergeant and scalded him so badly that he was absent in hospital for three months. After that he was sent back to the company for duty.

Of course he wasn't safe to put in any place except on some fatigue duty, and there he was left-handed, and never could tell whether a thing was anywhere near plumb, square, or level by looking at it.

Hake was a corker, and, as the boys used to say, "born in the wrong of the moon." Of course he had malaria and shakes, camp distemper, itch, fleas, and all that sort of thing. You never knew anything of that kind to skip the galoot.

At first I used to study him as one of the seven wonders of the world. Then, as his traits began to show themselves as something peculiarly and wonderfully different from everything else in nature, I began to admire him. He was unique. But after a while I found out another peculiarity. Whatever else was wrong, the man's heart was all right; not the least doubt about that.

Well, we kept him along with us in some way or other, not daring to let him go into any kind of fight for fear he would break everything all up in some unaccountable way, until we had the Deep Bottom fight in August, 1864. When we were along near Crow's Nest, someone from the ranks sung out:

"Worden, by the Lord Harry, I've forgotten my cartridge-box!"

It was Hake, and there he was, expecting to be in a fight any minute, and not a cartridge to his name. It was against orders but I skurried back to the baggage wagon and got him a cartridge box with 80 rounds, and just got back and handed them to him as the Johnnies let loose.

PRIVATE JOHN C. LANG
100TH ILLINOIS INFANTRY

Lang made these comments about the braggart who never kept up with the colors at a reunion held in September 1886 at Joliet, Illinois, the town where the 100th Illinois first mustered on August 30, 1862. As part of the Army of the Cumberland, the regiment fought at Murfreesboro, Chickamauga, Resaca, Kennesaw Mountain, and in the battles around Atlanta, in the Nashville campaign, and in numerous smaller engagements.

You were all acquainted with the soldier who was eternally spoiling for a fight, and who breakfasted regularly every day on a certain number of rebels killed by his own hand. You could not fail to know him, for his type was in every company, or at least in every regiment. His own bravery was the one subject of his ceaseless dis-

course, the one virtue he never tired of praising. How often around the campfire, at the picket post and on the march have you listened to the story of his valiant deeds, as related by himself. You knew he was a brave man and a good soldier, because he said so, but somehow you could never reconcile the fact with the manner in which he "panned out" when under fire. It was some time before you could realize that the most dangerous weapon such a soldier ever shot off was his mouth. I believe that I am talking now to as brave soldiers as ever shouldered a musket or wore a Government sock, but I do not believe that any one of you loved war for the mere sake of killing and being killed. Speaking for myself, and indirectly for all, I can say that in battle I always realized the danger to which I was exposed, and knew that I was as liable to be killed or crippled at any moment as the comrades who fell at my side. . . .

Some soldiers, as you all know by observation and experience, were more expert and accomplished foragers than others. It does not follow, however, that they were any better soldiers than their less successful comrades whose knowledge of the art of foraging was an acquired instead of a natural accomplishment. In fact, one of the best foragers I ever knew was of no account whatever as a soldier, except to stand guard and count as one when rations were issued. His accouterments were generally in good condition, his dress as neat and his kit as complete as possible, and he seemed as brave as the bravest when on parade or inspection, but I doubt if he ever fired a shot at the enemy during his three years' service, and he certainly did not allow the enemy to fire any at him, except at long range. He was the most finished specimen of the constitutional coward I ever met, and was only tolerated in the company on account of his general usefulness. Capt. Burrell repeatedly declared, with profane emphasis and hot indignation, that in the next fight this man should "face the music," but when the next fight took place Burrell always found something to do more important than looking after skulkers, and the fellow would pursue his usual tactics, retrograding so quietly and unostentatiously that no man could tell exactly when or where he dropped out of line.

The length of his absence would be regulated by the severity of the battle, but any time from 12 hours to two days after it was over he would turn up, serene, self-complacent and composed, with something good to eat in his haversack, and loaded to the muzzle with accounts of his wonderful exploits on some other part of the field, which he would relate with much volubility and great exactness as to time and place. The number of times his presence on a certain part of the battlefield saved the day to the Union army is represented by the number of engage-

"Like a flash of lightning the insulted youth had sprung to his feet, darted to the stack of arms, seized the Captain's sword, and slashed at Merrit's scalp!"

ments in which the regiment participated. Of course he served through the war, in his way, unharmed by disease and uninjured by rebel lead, for he always managed to be traveling so rapidly toward the rear when a battle commenced, that no bullet could possibly overtake him.

PRIVATE RANDOLPH A. SHOTWELL
8TH VIRGINIA INFANTRY

One of the miseries of soldiering, according to Shotwell, was having to live with "rough, uncouth fellows, whose mingled complaints, coarse jests, quarrels, noise and impatience make you sigh at the prospect of spending the entire day and the next, and the next and so on ad infinitum under precisely similar circumstances." The incident he retells here occurred in December 1861, when the regiment was wintering in Fairfax County, Virginia, and the men were idle and bored.

On the following day I returned to the main reserves, which were in the ruins of an old mill. In the detachment was a young man named Hutchinson, dark-skinned, moody, and strange looking, rarely speaking to anyone, and suspected of a hereditary disposition towards insanity.

Near him sat a young fellow named Merrit, a Baltimorean, whose only merit, that I ever observed, was embraced in his name. Besides being a physical coward he was a liar "when the truth would be better," and vulgar in word, thought, and action. He had drawn an obscene picture upon a piece of shingle, and handing it to Hutchinson, asked—"How do you like your Mother?"

Like a flash of lightning the insulted youth had sprung to his feet, darted to the stack of arms, seized the Captain's sword, and slashed at Merrit's scalp! With a blood-curdling scream the latter fled for his life, pursued closely by the maniac, whose stalwart arm hacked at his head, shoulders, and back at every bound! The act was so unexpected, and the cries of the flying wretch so startling, that few of us thought of interfering, though the man's life was in imminent peril.

Happily Captain Wampler, with more self-possession, seized a musket, and running across the arc of the circle, sprang between the lunatic, and Merrit just as the latter stumbled, and fell headlong—never to have risen again but for the brave Captain's interference. Hutchinson glared wildly at Wampler for an instant, but as the Captain's bayonet was almost at his heart, and as I, and others had now sprung to reinforce him,—there was no chance to resist. Slowly dropping the point of his weapon, he allowed his arms to be bound, and remained in moody sullenness until sent to a place of safety. He never recovered his sanity, I believe. Merrit was painfully slashed about his head and shoulders; but I am not sure he got a great deal of sympathy; as his obscenity caused the whole affair, and doubtless threw the unhappy youth's mind off the balance.

PRIVATE CARLTON MCCARTHY
2D COMPANY, RICHMOND HOWITZERS

The son of an Irish immigrant and a Virginia woman, McCarthy joined the Richmond Howitzers in 1864 at the age of 17 after his brother, an officer in the same battery, was killed at Cold Harbor. The following excerpt is taken from McCarthy's book, Detailed Minutiae of Soldier Life in the Army of Northern Virginia, which served as a Civil War textbook in the Virginia public schools for 20 years. McCarthy died in 1936 at the age of 89.

An accomplished straggler could assume more misery, look more horribly emaciated, tell more dismal stories of distress, eat more and march further (to the rear), than any ten ordinary men. Most stragglers were real sufferers, but many of them were ingenious liars, energetic foragers, plunder hunters and gormandizers. Thousands who kept their place in ranks to the very end were equally as tired, as sick, as hungry, and as hopeless, as these scamps, but too proud to tell it or use it as a means of escape from hardship.

Within a weeks time I & my officers start a school 1 1/2 hours per day for the men of the Company nearly one half of whom are ignorant of reading or writing. To read, to write (I shall not teach in this department) and a little ciphering will be our highest ambition. You know I am no advocate for education, specially for the masses, but there are many boys in the Company, some of them very bright and it seems my duty to do all I can for them, lest serving their Country should prevent them from acquiring such common & indispensable knowledge & so be a stumbling block forever to them. Besides they are Virginians and near of kin to me.

CAPTAIN JOHN H. CHAMBERLAYNE
PURCELL (VIRGINIA) ARTILLERY

Born in Richmond in 1838, the son of a prominent physician, "Ham," as he was known, grew up with an aristocratic perspective that included a powerful streak of noblesse oblige, as his words indicate. After the war he became one of the state's most influential newspaper editors, speaking out for reconciliation with the North.

PRIVATE ELI P. LANDERS
16TH GEORGIA INFANTRY

The ambrotype above was taken in Richmond in 1861 about the time Landers wrote the letter that follows to his mother, describing the statues of two American heroes he had seen in the Confederate capital. After surviving the carnage at Fredericksburg, Chancellorsville, and Gettysburg, Landers died of typhoid fever on October 27, 1863. He was 21 years old.

I got permission from my captain and went up in town. There I saw the greatest place I ever did see! Atlanta is nothing more than a kitchen to a Big House. I will tell you folks that there is no use in trying to compare nothing to what I have saw since I left home. I saw Washington's Monument. It was away up a stack of fine rock and he is on the largest horse that I ever saw. Washington is on the horse with his sword in his hand. The horse and man looks as natural as nature itself. Just get out of the way because it looks just like its coming right onto you! It is larger than any man or horse you ever saw I also shook hands with old Zachary Taylor yesterday evening. He looks just as natural as the man itself. It is about the size of a man and is made of tombstone. You can see the coat buttons and neck tie, even down to his shoe strings. Well, I really can't tell you as plain as it is. Here we are 750 miles apart and I am here trying to tell you the conditions!

A country boy away from home for the first time, Private Eli Landers discusses his efforts to find religion and avoid temptation in this letter to his mother back home in Gwinnett County, Georgia. Landers was writing in the winter of 1861 from Camp Cobb, located on the outskirts of Richmond and within easy reach of the city's many enticements.

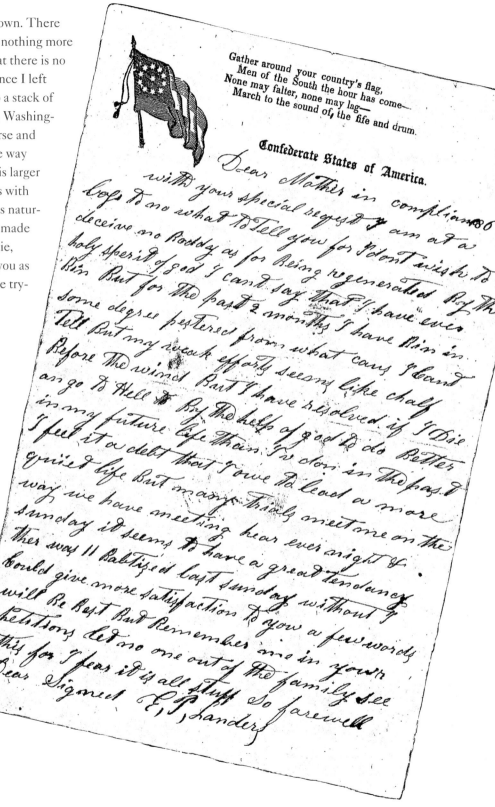

CAPTAIN THOMAS G. ORWIG
1ST PENNSYLVANIA LIGHT ARTILLERY

A distinguished attorney from Philadelphia, Orwig was mustered into the Union army in June 1861 and resigned in September 1864 to work in President Abraham Lincoln's reelection campaign. His comments about the evils of liquor were borne out by the facts—excessive drinking was the cause of most of the courts-martial in the Union Army of the Potomac.

"For officers, in spite of their braid and tinsel, are only men and some of them very weak ones who should not be trusted to temptation."

I regret to confess there is much to be seen in the army that is disgusting and degrading. But the greatest bane is the monster vice *intemperance* and this, too, amongst the officers. It commences by social drinking. Many good men and officers of high rank, entertain the idea that they cannot be hospitable, or gentlemanly without offering something to drink. When they have nothing, which rarely occurs, they make the greatest apologies for the want of it. So of course it is fashionable to have it and to drink. And indeed it is very hard for a young man and junior officer to decline the *honor* of the hospitalities of his seniors and superiors. Imagine a Lieutenant refusing to drink with a General and you may judge of the resolution necessary to save young men in the army from the drunkards fate. When officers get drunk, their example loosens the restraints upon all subordinates and then of course there is insubordination and shameful failure. Indeed the logic of our lawmakers is wrong in allowing officers to have liquor while they deny it to the rank and file. If it is not good for the privates it is not good for the officers, and *vice versa*. For officers, in spite of their braid and tinsel, are only men and some of them very weak ones who should not be trusted to temptation. I think there should be no intoxicating liquors in the army, excepting in the same way that arsenic is allowed—to be used as a medicine and dispensed by the surgeons. Those of my friends and acquaintances who used it as a preventative of disease, have weakly yielded to its seductive influences and are now, alas!, both morally and physically affected and on the dangerous road to ruin. An ounce of prevention, when it consists of whiskey, is not worth a pound of cure.

The straw-padded pocket liquor flask and telescoping silver cup were popular accouterments for officers in both the Federal and Confederate armies. The ready access to liquor enjoyed by officers was a source of much resentment from the enlisted men, who could enjoy its comforts only on the sly.

His tent flaps raised to let in the breeze, Lieutenant Colonel Samuel W. Owen of the 3d Pennsylvania Cavalry dozes through a hot afternoon at Harrison's Landing on the James River in July 1862, during the lull following General McClellan's Peninsula campaign. The liquor bottle on his cot was probably placed there by a mischievous onlooker who wanted to make it appear that Owen had overindulged.

SERGEANT HENRY G. ORR

12TH TEXAS CAVALRY

A young farmer who migrated from Tennessee to Ellis County, Texas, Henry was one of four Orr brothers to fight for the Confederacy. He served in eastern and southern Arkansas and in northern and central Louisiana. The ration of holiday whiskey, called Thompson's Eyewater by the Texans, was purchased in Houston by the regiment's officers.

December 25th, 1861: Christmas in camps. Before Aurora had dawned, the campfire was burning brightly and before "Sol" had smiled upon the encampment, the 4th Cavalry was seen with their shiny caps in hand marching up or grouped around the "center of attraction," impatiently awaiting to slake their thirst at the "sparkling bowl." The Colonel's fire served to elicit the largest crowd, and but few refused to participate in drinking toasts. Most everybody was more or less merry and some became "groggy." However, it only got the upper hand of two of the Rangers and exerted a very lively influence over them the greater portion of the day. Noon: the Colonel gave a dinner to the captains and commanding officers, and the orderly sergeants also dined at the second table. After dinner, the captains first and then commanding officers had to come up to the table one at a time and drink a toast, after which many of them were called upon to say something upon the occasion, the soldiers having drawn near.

Head Quarters 18th Army Corps,
Department of Virginia and North Carolina.

GENERAL ORDERS, }
No. 19. }   FORT MONROE, VA., *February 11th,* 1864.

To diminish drunkenness; to suppress tippling shops and ale houses, and to prevent affrays, brawls, and disorders arising therefrom—
It is ordered:

I....That all sales and deliveries, by traders, sutlers, or other persons, of intoxicating liquors from any booth, tent, or in any other shop or place of business, to be drunk upon the premises, are forbidden, under penalty of fine and imprisonment at hard labor.

II....Intoxicating liquors may be sold to be carried away by duly authorized druggists and apothecaries, upon the prescription of a licensed practising physician or surgeon, for medical purposes; by duly authorized hotel-keepers and victualers to their guests, to be used in their rooms, or with their meals, but any bar-room or tippling room, for the drinking of intoxicating liquors, is strictly forbidden.

By duly authorized grocers and dealers, to be carried away in quantities not less than a quart—if not the usually bottled liquors—and then not less than a bottle, nor more than five (5) gallons, or two cases of bottled liquors or wines, to any one person or family, within any period of ten (10) days, except one authorized dealer may sell to another, in any quantity, for the purpose of re-sale.

III....Every person authorized to sell liquor to be carried away will keep a true and accurate record of the person to whom, with his place of residence and occupation, time when, quantity, price and kind of liquor sold at each sale, in a book for that purpose, which is to be at all times open for inspection.

IV....Authorizations to sell as druggists, hotel keepers, victuallers, and dealers in liquors, may be obtained by the recommendation of Post and Sub-District Commanders, from the Provost Marshal at these Head Quarters, and at the Head Quarters of the District of North Carolina.

V....Any sale or delivery of liquor, by any person, contrary to this order, will be punished by confiscation of the stock in trade of the owner of the liquor sold or delivered, and the imprisonment at hard labor of the person making the sale, and the purchaser.

This general order against drinking, issued by the Confederate War Department on February 11, 1864, was originally drafted by Major General Braxton Bragg, then commanding troops in North Carolina. It failed to achieve its purpose. Later in the war Bragg would lament, "We have lost more valuable lives at the hands of the whiskey sellers than by the balls of our enemies."

SERGEANT GORHAM COFFIN
19TH MASSACHUSETTS INFANTRY

A shoemaker from West Newbury, Massachusetts, Coffin was wounded at Antietam on September 17, 1862, and killed at Gettysburg on July 3, 1863—decapitated by a cannonball, according to family lore. Coffin had risen to the rank of sergeant at the time of his death. He wrote the following excerpt in December 1861 while serving in the provost guard in Rockville, Maryland, which was charged with preventing "grog shops" from selling liquor to Federal troops.

The village contains eight hundred inhabitants. It has six churches: Congregationist, Baptist, Methodist, Catholic, Cambellite and Christian baptist, a female seminary, three taverns, courthouse and jail and any number of grog shops. We are here to guard the rum shops to prevent soldiers from obtaining liquor, to examine the passes of soldiers passing to and from Washington, and to keep things straight generally. Our duties are not hard. We now have seven posts to guard. No soldier is allowed to purchase a drop of liquor except by Capt. Merritt permission and no citizen is allowed to carry away more than a pint at a time. The arrangement does not suit all round but we make ourselves at home wherever we are, take the best seat in the bar room and *smell* all suspected jugs and bottles. It is something new to me to hang around grog shops but there is nothing like getting used to anything.

PRIVATE ISAAC N. DANIELS
37TH ALABAMA INFANTRY

Daniels enlisted in the Confederate army on March 17, 1862, at the age of 18. He was captured at Vicksburg in 1863 but was paroled soon afterward. He remained on active duty until April 26, 1865, when his unit surrendered to General William T. Sherman in North Carolina. In 1896 Daniels recounted this story about how he and his mates captured a barrel of whiskey.

You know how soldiers are any how, they are just like one of these little no-account fice dogs, you know they can't go any where but what they have to run round and get their nose into everything they can find. That's exactly like my company, or a part of it any how was, in the army. Well, you see, we had been on a march and hadn't had time to run over the country much and some of us were getting mighty dry, we wanted liquor, and we wanted it bad.

Well, we struck camp, along sorter in the shank of the evening, and some of us with rambling dispositions sailed out to see who and what was in the neighborhood. Directly we struck a railroad and hadn't gone far before we found the depot. It was over here at ——, Ga. Well, sir, in that depot there was liquor, barrel upon top of barrel. We knowed right then that we were going to have some of it, but to get it was the question. It was guarded by about eight soldiers, Georgia militia we called them. . . .

. . . Well, we went back to camp and told the boys what we had found. We had a man in our company from Virginia, and if ever he had any name but "Toddy" from Virginia, I never heard of it. Toddy said, said he, boys if you will get up a squad of eight men and I can get a lieutenant's coat, belt and sword, we will have some of that liquor, and it won't be long first either. He went to get the coat and I went to get the men. It was only a few minutes before he was back and the men were ready. He put on that coat and told us to fall in, which we did. You ought to have seen him, he would have walked over a colonel. He was the biggest man with an officer's coat on that I ever saw. He didn't ask anybody any odds. Well, sir, he marched us down to the depot and relieved the militia and sent them to their camps. Before they were out of sight good we had a barrel of whisky and was gone with it. We knew that as soon as they reached camps the officers would send them back faster than they left. . . .

. . . Several of the boys got drunk before night. As soon as night came we sailed out with every canteen in the company for our barrel, and

"A shipment of beer was left on the freight platform one night with a guard over it named Arnold."

among the crowd was old man Make Ellis. The first thing I knew he came up with a wash pot that would hold about fifteen gallons, he filled that pot and put it on his head and carried it near the camps, we then went and woke up the boys and led the way to the pot. When ever we found one of the men that was disposed to make too much fuss we would whisper "liquor" in his ear and that was all that was necessary. Some one had a little tin cup and after we had formed a circle around the pot that cup started on the circuit. A fellow would reach in the pot and get a drink and pass it to the next man and by the time it got back to him he was ready for more. Occasionally one would take a notion to go to camps, but he didn't walk like a man, he crawled off on all fours, and some of them could not do that even.

SERGEANT CHARLES C. HASKELL
16TH VERMONT INFANTRY

A 27-year-old schoolteacher from Wilmington, Vermont, Haskell began a nine-month enlistment on October 23, 1862. He was on fatigue duty at Fairfax Station, Virginia, with a squad from his regiment when the battle-tested 13th Pennsylvania Reserves (called the Bucktails because each member wore a buck's tail on his hat) arrived by train and staged a raid on the sutler's tent.

Some of the Bucktails, as soon as they broke ranks, began to look around for "wet goods," which they soon found at the Sutler's. Officers advised the Sutler not to let the men have any more. This angered the Reserves. Soon the tent pins of the Sutler's tent began to fly out; the tent collapsed. The boys went under and soon came out with quantities of such articles as they could lay their hands on. One of them had a pair of boots under one arm and ginger cakes in both hands. Another had a cheese under one arm, from which the boys began to help themselves. The last I saw the fellow had the rim.

When the Sutler saw that he was doomed, he rolled out a barrel of whisky. The boys knocked in the head. A few only who were near the barrel could get any. Those who had their cups full could not get away. The surging went on till the barrel was pushed over and the whisky spilled on the ground, which had recently frozen in ruts and foot marks, from which the boys began to try to get their share. Such a noise and commotion you never heard except from these Pennsylvanians. The long roll was sounded and the Bucktails and Reserves were gathered together and marched toward Fairfax Court House.

PRIVATE WILLIAM E. BEVENS
1ST ARKANSAS INFANTRY

Bevens enlisted in the Confederate army on May 5, 1861, at Jacksonport, Tennessee. He was serving under the command of Lieutenant Colonel M. Jeff Thompson, the self-styled Missouri Swamp Fox, when Thompson surrendered his force to Major General Grenville M. Dodge, commander of the Department of Missouri, in May 1865.

Sometimes a company would buy a barrel of oysters, take it to their hut and open it, and find in the center a five gallon jug of red rye. It was so concealed to pass the provost guard on [the] train. But the boys did even worse. Seven of them from other commands, went to Fredericksburg, bought a coffin and filled it with jugs. With sad faces and measured steps they carried it solemnly to the train. But the joke was too good to keep. The boys unscrewed the lid and yelled at the guard. Of course, when the train returned no one could name the offenders.

CORPORAL THOMAS W. MOFFATT
12TH ILLINOIS INFANTRY

Born in Orillia, Ontario, Moffatt moved to Amboy, Illinois, as a child. He enlisted in the army in 1861 at the age of 17. Moffatt was on guard duty in Corinth, Mississippi, when this incident occurred, demonstrating the boundless ingenuity of thirsty soldiers and the willingness of sympathetic officers to look the other way.

A shipment of beer was left on the freight platform one night with a guard over it named Arnold. That night Bill Caldwell, a member of our company, got hold of an auger somewhere and crept under the platform armed with the auger and a few pails. A small squad of eager volunteers lent aid and assistance.

Bill proceeded to bore holes here and there where he judged the barrels of beer were and soon his efforts were rewarded by a downpour of that liquid. One after another the pails were filled and the men went staggering up the track with them to where they were eagerly awaited by the rest of the men who were in on the deal. One would think that in a case of this kind the men would become intoxicated but in truth there was very little of the beer drunk and it was lying around by the pailful when the investigation was made next day. Notwithstanding the fact that pails of beer were in plain sight smelling to heaven and swarming with flies, the officers failed to discover any signs of beer in camp and nothing came of the investigation. I suppose they decided that the escapade was more of an expression of unbridled spirits than a breach of discipline so they winked when their eyes were turned in the direction of the evidence of our guilt.

Below, men of the provost marshal's command stand amid the ruins of a shop they destroyed in Alexandria, Virginia, by order of Brigadier General John P. Slough, military governor. The owner had been selling liquor to Union troops. Bad whiskey had killed several Union soldiers in Alexandria and had sickened many others.

LIEUTENANT ABNER R. SMALL
16TH MAINE INFANTRY

Small answered President Lincoln's first call for volunteers in April 1861, joining the 3d Maine. After the Union defeat at Bull Run that year, he returned to his home state as a recruiting officer and raised the 16th Maine. The following incident took place near Mitchell's Station on the Orange & Alexandria Railroad near Culpeper, Virginia, on December 31, 1863.

When we turned up on our calendar the last day of the year, we were still stuck in the mud, in a cheerless and exposed position on the extreme front of the army. It was a stated day for our being mustered for pay. Major Leavitt was assigned to muster the 39th Massachusetts, and Lieutenant-Colonel Peirson of that regiment was to muster the 16th Maine. Our men, frozen and muddy, were not in temper for ceremony, but regulations required an inspection before the muster and a review before the inspection.

I had the bugler sound the call; our companies turned out under arms; but the band, which should have assembled, was nowhere to be seen. I had the call repeated; still no band. Then I went up to the right, found the trouble, and fell into temptation.

"Mr. Shea, did you hear the call?"

John Shea was always a gentleman. He doffed his hat and managed to say slowly and politely:

"A'jutant, I hope you'll 'xcuse me; I'm drunk."

"How's the B flat, Mr. Shea?"

"He's bad off's I am."

"And how's the bass?"

"Dre'ful tired; 's lain down."

"Are any of you sober?"

"Well, I'd say, A'jutant, we simply shouldn' play."

"Oh, nonsense! There's a cold spring of water down there. Send for

a pailful or two, bathe your heads, and drink a quart of it, every one of you, and you'll be all right. Hurry up!"

I returned to my quarters, thinking of what would happen when the water should get warm. A few minutes later I heard the notes of "Adjutant's Call," clear and correct. The band, all present, played the companies into line. On notice from me, the captain of the first company stepped a pace to the front and gave the command:

"Orders—arms! Parade—rest!"

From captain to captain down the line the order was repeated, and smartly obeyed by the men. All right so far. But now the band was to march, playing, down the front of the line and back again. With some misgiving, I ordered:

"Troop—beat off!"

Away went the band, and the ground seemed very uneven under its feet; and now and then the leader would lose a note and, trying to catch it, would clash into the B flat; and the bass drum persisted in coming down heavy on the up beat; and the cymbals forgot to clang when they should, and closed with a crash when they should have been still. The musicians, countermarching, started in quick time together; but now the water was warm, and somehow the orders of Mr. Shea were not understood, and half the band struck up one tune, the other half another. This was too much. I heard above the discord a loud and angry voice:

"Parade is dismissed!"

PRIVATE JAMES GREENALCH
1ST MICHIGAN ENGINEERS

A carpenter by trade, Greenalch had been a soldier for only a month when he wrote the following letter to his wife, Fidelia, and her parents, describing the army's harsh treatment of drunken soldiers. He served for nearly three years, participating in the battles around Atlanta and in Sherman's march through Georgia and the Carolinas.

Sept. 28, 1862
Lewisville, Kentucky
Dear Parents and Wife,
We have just arrived in Camp. We stayed two nightets and one day in the convalesancet Baricks at the city and I can tell you I saw in that time what I never saw before in my life and hope and pray I never shall

"Away went the band, and the ground seemed very uneven under its feet; and now and then the leader would lose a note and, trying to catch it, would clash into the B flat."

again. We ware put on gourd the next morning after we got there, two hours on and four off, and the last night it came my lot and Nates to tend the gourd house. Our first tower [tour] was the worst, it was in the first part of the evening, some fifteen or twenty drunk and some not, and fetching them in all the time holering and swaring, some of them the officers, two or three of them, would pitch on one man and knock him down and pound him all up, some of them handcofed and some tied down to the benches groaning and yeling. They made so much disturbance and noise that one of the oficers went out and got a revolver and pointed it at two or three of them and told them if they did not sit down and be still he would give them the contence. Last night two men were shot by the goard. They were told to stop and did not and they fired. They were drunk I sopose. One was shot dead, the other was brought in to the hospital this morning, and another was shot the night before. They ware our men and shot by our men, that was their orders. Yesterday morning, I helped to cary out a dead man that was poisend, had not ben dead onely about two hours and the foam poryed from his moith and smelt so that none of them wanted to help cary him out, it is suposed he was poisend by some secech. I tell you it was a leson to me, did I not see the evel of sin and the beauty of religeon.

Union soldiers being disciplined for drunkenness stand tethered to trees while their guards lounge beside them in this sketch by Alfred R. Waud. Two of the men have been gagged with bayonets. Other common army punishments included having to march all day while wearing a barrel or carrying a musket and a knapsack weighted down with stones.

PRIVATE GEORGE DRAKE
85TH ILLINOIS INFANTRY

Drake ran away from home to join the Union forces in July 1862 at the age of 16. The photograph above was taken shortly afterward. When his parents fretted about the corrupting influences of army life on their son's morality, George reassured them in a letter. "I never regret the day that I enlisted," he wrote, "for if I had staid out of the army and went to school all the time I would not of learned half so mutch. That is about war and men and the principles of some men."

Wednesday morning March 29, 1865
Campt Goldsboro North Carolina
Dear Parents. . . .

You spoke about generals ought to be good moral Christian men but the most of them are very wicked and when they get into action they will cuss and sware.

A battle is the greatest place for swearing in the world. For when one party gets the other to a retreat they will cuss them and holler halt. At Chickamauga I know when we had to move one morning the rebbels were rite on our heels and followed us on the run hollering, "Halt you dambed Yankys. . . .

I remain your son as ever
George

LIEUTENANT ALBERT T. GOODLOE
35TH ALABAMA INFANTRY

Goodloe spoke for many Civil War soldiers when he wrote this reminiscence about the pleasures of tobacco. After leaving Port Hudson, Louisiana, in April 1863, one month before the beginning of the Federal siege, Goodloe and his comrades wintered in Mississippi, then joined the Army of Tennessee, seeing action in the battles around Atlanta and in Hood's failed Tennessee campaign.

When not on duty we were kept quite close in our quarters by severely cold or rainy weather, and then it was that we enjoyed in an especial manner the improvements that we had made, those of us who had taken the pains to make any. I call to mind how those of us who used tobacco relished our pipes when thus confined to our camp tenements by inclement weather. I have long been opposed to the use of the "weed" in any way, but in those days I esteemed such indulgence next to a necessity, and an inexpressible delight. January 20, 1863, while in camp at Grenada, Miss., I wrote in my diary, expecting thereafter to make it more full: "Here I must insert an essay when I have leisure on the luxury of the pipe in camp in cold weather." This was while we were having some very cold, disagreeable weather. We had a great deal of rain while in camp on Big Black in

Tennessee cavalry soldiers, three of them tugging on their ever-present
pipes, pose for a keepsake photograph with their body servants. The trooper
seated on the right carries a tobacco bag attached to a button on his tunic.
A popular fad among Confederate soldiers, such bags, usually decorated,
were generally gifts from mothers, wives, or sweethearts.

February, 1863, and in my diary of the 13th of that month occurs this utterance: "O the luxury of a pipe in camp! Would that the Muses would inspire me to write a poetical essay on that subject!" It is too late for such a performance as that now, were I ever so poetical, which I am not, there being no poetry to me in the pipe in these times of peace. Several of us had joined in a smoke together that day, and at the conclusion of it resolutions were passed requesting whoever could to write of the value of the pipe under such circumstances, but none of us felt competent to do the subject justice.

My recollection is that most of the soldiers with whom I was thrown from time to time both chewed and smoked tobacco as a constant habit, whether in camp or on the march, but one of them, not of our immediate command, whom I met in North Alabama in the winter of 1864, gave me this hint on the tobacco habit, which I here record as a *Rebel relic:*

Tobacco is a noxious weed.
Davy Crockett sowed the seed.
It robs your pocket and soils your clothes,
And makes a chimney of your nose.

SERGEANT DANIEL ELDREDGE
3D NEW HAMPSHIRE INFANTRY

Eldredge describes how Yankee ingenuity made up for the shortage of matches and pipes on Hilton Head Island, South Carolina. A native of Lebanon, New Hampshire, he survived dysentery and two wounds—in the foot at Fort Wagner, South Carolina, in 1863, and in the left forearm at Deep Bottom Run in 1864. During the last months of the war he ran an induction center in his home state.

Private C. W. Farnum of Company F, 6th New Hampshire Infantry, brought this plug of chewing tobacco back with him from the South, where he fought in Virginia. When Yankee pickets fraternized with their Rebel counterparts, they often exchanged their good coffee for aromatic Southern tobacco.

Cotton though plenty at that time, soon became scarce, and was in great demand. This demand was supplied from the wadding in our caps, which were made of a peculiar pattern by Messrs. Purinton & Ham of Dover, N.H. The cause of this great demand was a scarcity of matches. Pipes must be lighted and the smokers could be seen transferring a piece of lighted cotton from pipe to pipe until quite consumed. Only one match was necessary for a large body of smokers.

The sweet briar wood grows on Hilton Head in great abundance and was soon discovered by the Yankee soldier. Pipes of curious devices, carved well and ill, soon flooded the market and nearly every man whether smoker or anti-tobacconist had a sweet briar pipe cut and carved by his own hand. For the benefit of the uninformed I will state that the sweet briar is a root and a clambering vine. The root is the part from which pipes are made. It grows in no regular shape, being composed of a series of bunches of all sizes, from a walnut to six inches in diameter, of all shapes imaginable so that one can find something from which to make any model he chooses. In its green state it is white but as it grows old and partly dead it is hard and of the color of a reddish brick.

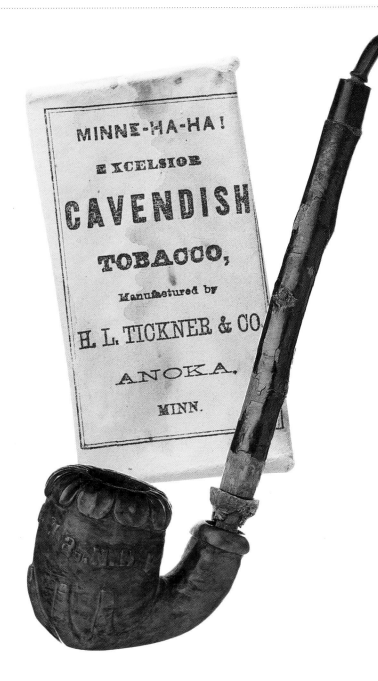

LIEUTENANT BROMFIELD L. RIDLEY

STAFF, MAJOR GENERAL ALEXANDER P. STEWART

Ridley describes how humor helped keep him cheerful. A teenager when he left the Nashville Military Academy to enlist, Ridley helped capture 200 retreating Federals at Murfreesboro on December 31, 1862. After serving in General John Hunt Morgan's cavalry, he joined the staff of General Stewart, fighting at Chickamauga, in defense of Atlanta, and in Hood's disastrous Tennessee expedition.

The pipe above was carved out of sweetbrier root on Hilton Head Island, South Carolina, by Private T. Adams, one of Daniel Eldredge's fellow soldiers in the 3d New Hampshire Infantry. The Federals' tobacco usually came in small packets like the one above, manufactured by a Minnesota firm.

And now I will while away a few of the hours of armistice by transcribing some of the Nomenclature of our Southern Armies: The North Carolinians are called "Tar Heels;" South Carolinians, "Rice Birds;" Georgians, "Goober Grabbers;" Alabamians, "Yaller Hammers;" Texans, "Cow Boys;" Tennesseans, "Hog Drivers;" Louisianians, "Tigers;" Floridians, "Gophers;" Virginians, "Tobacco Worms;" Arkansans, "Tooth-picks;" Missourians, "Border Ruffians;" Kentuckians, "Corn Crackers;" and Mississippians, "Sand Lappers." The Cavalry, "Buttermilk Rangers;" Infantry, "Webfoot." A regiment of deserters from the Federal Army, kept behind by us to build forts, "Galvanized Rebs." The Federals called us "Johnnies;" we called them "Yanks" and "Blue Bellies."

See a fellow with a Bee Gum hat ride down a line, "He's a gentleman from the States." The soldiers guy him with such remarks as "Come out of that hat. I know you are thar; see your toes wigglin'." If boots are long and big, they will say, "See your head stickin' out." In passing a troop in camp, a number will look up a tree and halloo, "Come out of that tree. See you up thar." This attracts, and then the laugh comes. In camp, when all is still, the monotony is broken by some forager making a hog squeal. His fellows cry out, "I'll kill any man's hog that bites me." A cavalryman, passing infantry, is accosted with "Jump off and grab a root." A by-word of the soldiers—"I havn't had a square meal for three days." Soldiers in camp say to soldiers going to the front, "You'd better gim me that hat; you'll lose it out thar.". . .

I got hold of a silver crescent on the Dalton Campaign, placed it on the left side of my hat, put on a biled shirt and a paper collar, and rode down Division line. They began on me, "Ahem! Umph! Umph! Biled shirt! Ladies' man! Parlor ornament! Take him to his ma!"

On the march to Tennessee, the officer who would get them out of the sorghum patches caught it. They'd say, "Boys, there goes old Sorghum."

In Cavalry, Number Four invariably held horses in battle. It was such a delightful number that when it fell upon a soldier, he would say, "Bully!" Col. Paul Anderson changed the mirth by saying, "Boys, Number One will hold horses, and you 'Bullies' will dismount.". . .

It carried you back to old times to hear the guards around a regiment halloo out, "T-w-e-l-v-e o'-c-l-o-c-k and a-l-l's well!" The rude and untrained soldier would play on that and say, "T-w-e-l-v-e o'-c-l-o-c-k, and as sleepy as H——l!" When a soldier goes out foraging, it is called "Going on a lark;" when he goes stealing, it is "Impressing it into service;" when a Quartermaster wants to shield his rascality, he has a favorite abstract called "L," which is used, and means "Lost in the service;" when a squad runs from the enemy, it is "Skedaddling;" the ricochetting of a cannon ball is "Skiugling"—words whose origin began with this war. Let a stranger or soldier enter camp and call for a certain company—say, Company F. Some soldier will say, "Here's Company F!" By the time he can get there, another will cry out at the far part of the regiment, "Here's Company F!" Then the whole command will take up the refrain, until the poor fellow in vexation will sulk away. Let an old soldier recognize a passing friend, and say, "How are you, Jim?" a marching division will keep it up, with "How are you, Jim?" until the poor fellow swoons.

In the army we have some of the finest mimics in the world. Let one cackle like a hen, and the monotony of camp is broken by the encore of "S-h-o-o!" Then other cacklers take it up, until it sounds like a poultry yard stirred up over a mink or weasel. Let one bray like an ass, others take it up until the whole regiment will personate the sound, seemingly like a fair ground of asses.

SERGEANT VALERIUS C. GILES
4TH TEXAS INFANTRY

In the summer of 1861 the 19-year-old Giles left the family farm just outside Austin to join the Tom Green Rifles, a militia group that became part of John Bell Hood's hard-fighting Texas Brigade. There were a good many card sharks in the brigade, especially poker players who, Giles recollected, "managed to keep the novices and greenhorns pretty well strapped."

I got a pass from Lieutenant James T. McLaurin to visit my brother, W. L. Giles, Mike Hornsby, and several other old friends who belonged to the Sixth Texas Infantry of Granberry's Brigade. They were camped at the foot of Missionary Ridge, about three miles from our camp at Lookout Mountain. Just before reaching their camp I came to "Gambler's Paradise." It was an open space containing two or more acres, trampled hard and smooth as a floor. Fly tents and brush arbors dotted the ground in every direction, while hundreds of men were congregated there engaged in every imaginable game of chance known to the Confederate soldier, from chuck-a-luck to faro.

These men came from every part of the army and represented every branch of the service. Stool pigeons were calling like auctioneers, proclaiming the merits and fairness of their games.

"Here's the place to get your money back."

"Right this way, gentlemen! You put down a dollar and pick up a V."

Heads you win, tails I loose," and so forth.

Suckers were thick, and bit like garfish. Great rolls of Old Confed lay on blankets and rudely constructed tables. Here and there you could see small stacks of half dollars, quarters and dimes, but no gold was in sight.

It was "Paradise Lost" to many a poor devil who blew in the last cent he had and then trudged back to his regiment, busted but no wiser.

Gambling—usually on dice and card games but also on contests of all sorts, including footraces, cockfights, boxing matches, and baseball games—was a favorite pastime in army camps both North and South. Gambling was sometimes banned by local commanders. In this Alfred Waud sketch, two Union soldiers found in violation are forced to play dice for pebbles until they collapse from exhaustion. The sketch was made near Bristoe Station, Virginia, in October 1863.

Tenting Tonight

At the beginning of the war some privileged militia units enjoyed a life of luxury in their encampments, with the amenities of home and hearth readily available. Some units even employed professional chefs to oversee their meals. The Washington Artillery of New Orleans hired a French cook who had worked in one of that city's finest restaurants. "Ah!" Lieutenant William M. Owen remembered, "he was *magnifique.*" When Philadelphia lawyer Charles Collis organized a colorfully uniformed company called the Zouaves d'Afrique, he recruited an Italian chef named Nunzio Finelli, hailed as "the best cook in the army." While preparing gourmet dishes— omelette soufflés were his specialty—Finelli would regale the officers mess with operatic arias. But the hardships of active campaigning soon put an end to such culinary extravagance.

Most volunteers, accustomed to home-cooked meals, found themselves on their own when it came to the preparation of rations. Some units, such as Private Edgar Warfield's company of the 17th Virginia, divided into messes of two dozen or more men. Much to Warfield's disappointment, he soon discovered that the designated cooks "knew no more about cooking than a man who had never seen a frying pan or skillet." One batch of flapjacks proved so inedible that the irate Virginians nailed them to the trees beside their camp. When the regiment passed that way six months later, the flapjacks were still there.

Soldiers could occasionally vary their menu by purchasing food from local civilians or patronizing the traveling vendors called sutlers. While camped near Richmond, Private William A. Fletcher of the 5th Texas noted, "We bought about everything that was offered, without question, if it suited our fancy." Sausage was a popular item with Fletcher and his pards until, as he recalled, "I found what I supposed was a cat's claw and all stopped eating at once and an examination was hurriedly made of the uneaten portion, and a cat's tooth was discovered." Fletcher remembered, "Some of the boys tried to vomit, but the cat kept on its downward course,

Federal army butchers weigh rations of meat under the watchful eyes of a commissary at Camp Essex in northern Virginia. Regulations mandated a daily issue of 20 ounces of salt beef or 12 ounces of salt pork. The meat, dubbed salt horse by the soldiers, was packed in brine sufficient to preserve it for two years.

Tin cups, such as this decorated version that belonged to Corporal Frank D. Ruggles of the 1st Company, Washington Artillery of New Orleans, served as drinking vessel, soup bowl, and occasionally as an entrenching tool. A comrade incised the battery's badge and an inscription as a memorial to Ruggles, who was killed at Fredericksburg in 1862.

so their was a slump in the sausage market."

In an era when food processing and preservation was still in the experimental stage, the Union and Confederate commissaries were faced with the challenge of supplying rations that were resistant to spoilage and easily transported by armies in the field. While fresh cuts of beef, loaves of soft bread, and fresh vegetables could be issued to troops stationed in a semipermanent camp or garrison, soldiers on campaign were compelled to subsist upon field rations carried in their haversack—a monotonous and unpalatable diet of coffee, hard bread, and salted meat, usually pork.

Coffee proved to be the most popular item on the army menu. It was generally issued as unground beans that the men crushed with a rock, gun butt, or bayonet, then boiled in their tin cups. "Coffee could not be dispensed with," wrote Lewis Bissell of the 2d Connecticut Heavy Artillery; "I don't know how I could get along without it on a long march." When the Northern blockade of Southern ports restricted Confederate access to coffee, Rebel soldiers frequently had to rely upon a variety of unpopular vegetable substitutes such as burned wheat and chicory.

The standard army bread supplied to Federal troops was a square flour-and-water biscuit, dubbed hardtack for its rocklike consistency. Hardtack became more palatable if soaked in water and fried in the sizzling fat of the issue salt pork—"sowbelly" in soldier parlance. Occasionally the hardtack was found to be infested with weevils—or "squirmers." Pennsylvania officer Frederick Hitchcock recalled, "It came to be a rule to eat in daylight for protection against the unknown quantity in the hardtack. If we had to eat in the dark, after a prolonged march, our protection then lay in breaking our cracker into a cup of boiling coffee, stir it well and then flow enough of the coffee over to carry off most of the strangers and take the balance on faith."

Confederate soldiers often grated corn to make a crude form of bread that, though fresher than hardtack, was equally monoto-

nous when eaten for weeks or months at a time. "We have had nothing but bacon & corn bread," 24th Alabama colonel Newton Davis wrote in the summer of 1864; "I fear that if it is continued much longer we will all have the scurvy. The soldiers are all crazy for vegetables." In their longing for greens, some of Davis' men ate potato vines. As shortages increased, many Southern fighting men went without meat for days at a stretch. South Carolinian Berry Benson counted himself lucky to subsist on a handful of parched corn and some green apples. He had seen comrades "reduced to the extremity of picking grains of corn out of the horses' dung, washing it, and parching it for food."

It was no wonder that most soldiers, Yank and Reb alike, chose to supplement their diet by foraging off the countryside. John Robson of the 52d Virginia thought it "no uncommon sight to see a whole brigade marching in solid column along a road one minute and the next scattered over a big briar field picking the blackberries." Orders prohibiting the theft of private property were generally of little avail in safeguarding pigs, chickens, corn, and sweet potatoes from the voracious appetites of the fighting men. Many officers chose to turn a blind eye to their soldiers' transgressions. Many Federal commanders resorted to organized foraging as a means of sustaining their armies on campaign—a military necessity, but one that held dire consequences for the civilian population.

His horse draped with chickens foraged from nearby farms, Private Billy Crump, an orderly on the staff of Colonel Rutherford B. Hayes of the 23d Ohio Infantry, returns to his camp in western Virginia. In one memorable foraging expedition, Crump netted 50 chickens, two turkeys, one goose, 20 dozen eggs, and more than 30 pounds of butter.

Whether they hailed from farm or city, most Civil War volunteers quickly learned that life in camp was rough, dirty, and filled with hardships. "I have not shaved since I left home and I am almost burned black," Lieutenant James Edmondson wrote his wife a month after marching to war with the 27th Virginia; "we have to take the rain as it comes and sleep (if we can) on the damp ground with the water dripping on us from above." Even men accustomed to physical labor found their endurance sorely taxed by long marches, inadequate rations, and the discomforts of life in the open. Before most units ever fired a shot in anger, dozens of soldiers succumbed to diseases such as typhoid, dysentery, and measles, or were invalided home with rheumatism, chronic diarrhea, or a combination of symptoms the surgeons referred to as general debility.

Poor sanitation in the crowded army camps was a major cause of illness. Latrines, or "sinks," were often dug in proximity to the streams that served both for bathing and as a source of drinking water. Invariably some men were more conscientious than others when it came to personal hygiene. "Some of our boys are not over and above clean," Ohioan George Cadman noted, "and if not pretty sharply looked after would not wash themselves from weeks end to weeks end." Confederate soldier Randolph Shotwell never forgot his first introduction to the close con-

fines of a canvas tent: "The night was very hot and sultry," he wrote, "and the odor of seven pairs of unwashed feet filled the interior of the tent with nauseating oppressiveness."

Wearing the same dirty, sweat-stained woolen uniform for months at a time, and with only the occasional change of shirt and underclothing, every Civil War soldier came to know the discomfort of body lice, or graybacks as they were popularly known. "The feeling of intense disgust aroused by the first contact with these creepers soon gave way to hardened indifference," wrote Massachusetts artilleryman John D. Billings; "a soldier realized the utter impossibility of keeping free from them." Wilbur Hinman of the 65th Ohio

observed, "There were times when everybody, from generals down, 'had 'em' more or less, and no power on earth could prevent it."

"Skirmishing for graybacks" became a well-known army ritual, with dozens or even hundreds of semiclad soldiers pinching the lice between thumb and forefinger as they sat cross-legged on the ground. Maine officer Abner Small noted that "a graduate from Harvard and an illiterate from the wilds of Maine were often seen affectionately picking lice together." Some men chose to boil their clothes periodically but invariably became reinfested soon after. William Fletcher of the 5th Texas found that by holding his clothing over a campfire it was possible to smoke the

lice out. "If one was stocked with big fat fellows," he noted, "it would remind him of popping corn."

In addition to the ubiquitous graybacks, Sergeant Major Elbridge Copp of the 3d New Hampshire enumerated a variety of other insect pests, including chiggers, wood ticks, and sand fleas, concluding, "There were many things the soldiers suffered from, besides the enemy's bullets." Indiana lieutenant John Hadley thought the swarms of mosquitoes along Virginia's Rappahannock River rivaled even the graybacks, writing, "I never came in contact with such gigantic cannibals, such mammoth blood suckers, such unprincipled gluttons."

According to prewar army regulations, regiments were supposed to pitch their canvas tents in an orderly, geometric layout of parallel company streets. In their first months of service, most troops were quartered either in A tents—holding four to six men—or in conical Sibley tents, the design of which resembled an Indian tipi. Sibley tents were capable of housing a dozen, and sometimes as many as 18, soldiers. Most Sibleys were equipped with a stove, the pipe of which exited through a hole at the apex of the tent, and at night the men would sleep in a circular pattern around the central fire.

When troops were on the move, both A and Sibley tents had to be transported in wagons because of their size. The result was often a logistic nightmare in which many units were forced to bivouac without tentage because their regimental wagon trains were stuck in muddy roads miles to the rear when the time came to bed down. By early 1862 most military commanders realized that on campaign their soldiers would have to carry the necessities of life on their backs, and the so-called shelter tent, patterned on the French army's *tente d'abri,* became standard issue. Each soldier carried half of a tent—a piece of canvas about five feet square. When pitching camp two soldiers would button their halves together to create what came to be known as a dog tent or pup tent. If no trees were available from which to cut ridgepoles, the men would sometimes use their muskets as improvised supports. In good weather they might forgo the tent and sleep beside a campfire, wrapped in their blankets.

On campaign most encampments were haphazard affairs, rarely laid out according to regulations, and they could be broken down and moved at a moment's notice. Veteran soldiers learned to make do with less, and many were content to improvise tents from their rubber-coated ponchos or ground cloths. Others pooled their resources and constructed crude shelters of sticks and brush called shebangs. In cold weather a group of men would often share ponchos and blankets, bunching close together—or "spooning"—for warmth.

In time, experienced campaigners came to appreciate the humble pleasures of a bivouac in the field, what Major Peter Vredenburgh of the 14th New Jersey called "the sweets of soldier life." One October day in 1862 he wrote, "Our campfire is lit, and though beauty is absent, song and wit are there, flavored with the cracking of jokes and the crackling of hickory making one feel as if he was enjoying a clam bake or evening frolic at home instead of being here in the wilderness."

Major campaigns were rare in winter. It was a time for rest and refitting, a season to receive welcome packages from loved ones. The soldiers had time to obtain a measure of comfort by constructing log cabins that gave their vast encampments the appearance of a pioneer settlement. Virginian George S. Bernard described these winter huts as "strange looking houses, half logs, half canvas, with huge chimneys," and observed that "no two of them resembled each other in architecture." Usually sleeping four to six men and equipped with a fireplace, cots, or bunk beds—and sometimes even purloined rugs and window frames—the winter hut was the closest thing to a home most soldiers saw in their years at war. "Our shanty seemed a part of ourselves," remembered Charles Sprague of the 44th New York, "and of all the homes that I have ever loved and left there is none which has left so deep an impression as that little hut of one room, built of pine logs, sticks, sods, mud, and canvas."

This crate of army bread, or hardtack, was packed by Brooklyn baker Robert Stears and received by the U.S. Army Subsistence Department in September 1862. The simple flour-and-water biscuits were protected from moisture by a soldered sheet-zinc lining. Once issued, recalled Private Wilbur Fisk of the 2d Vermont, "hardtack suffered every indignity, and was positively unsuitable food for anything that claims to be human."

Camped near Pensacola, the Orleans Cadets—one of five new companies recruited to form the 1st Louisiana—pose for New Orleans photographer J. D. Edwards in the spring of 1861. With insufficient force to challenge the Federal fleet guarding nearby Fort Pickens, the Louisianans lazed away their short stay at Bayou Grande.

PRIVATE RANDOLPH A. SHOTWELL
8TH VIRGINIA INFANTRY

In November 1861, after the Battle of Ball's Bluff, Randolph Shotwell's regiment was ordered into winter quarters at Centreville, Virginia. There the young schoolboy turned soldier faced his first winter away from home and the comforts of civilian life. Shotwell reflected that later in the war "even the discomforts of Centreville would be recalled as positive luxuries."

Fancy the comforts of such a life as this! Roused at dawn to crawl out and stand half-dressed in a drenching storm while the company-roll was being called; then return to damp blankets—or to rub the skin off of your knuckles, trying to start a fire with green pine poles in the storm; go down to the marsh to break the ice off of a shal-low branch or rivulet, and flirt a few handfuls of muddy water upon your face, then wipe it off on the clean corner of a dirty pocket handkerchief, borrow a broken piece of comb (having lost your own, and having no money to replace it) and, after raking the bits of trash out of your stubby locks, devote the next hour to trying to boil a dingy tin-cup of so-called coffee; after which, with a chunk of boiled beef, or broiled bacon *(red,* almost, with rust and skippers) and a piece of cornbread, you are ready to breakfast. But now you have blackened your hands, and are begrimed with the sooty smoke from the snapping, popping, sappy, green pine logs, your eyes are red and smarting, your face burned while your back is drenched and chilled; and you have no place to sit while eating your rough meal.

Around you are dozens of rough, uncouth fellows, whose mingled complaints, coarse jests, quarrels, noise and impatience make you sigh at the prospect of spending the entire day and the next, and the next, and so on *ad infinitum* under precisely similar circumstances.

PRIVATE EDWARD MURRAY
96TH ILLINOIS INFANTRY

Answering the call to arms in September 1862, Edward Murray of Waukegan, Illinois, rented his farm to a neighbor, sold his team of horses, and bade farewell to his wife and six children. In the following month, his regiment left the Chicago area, where it had mustered, and crossed the Ohio River at Cincinnati to occupy the town of Covington, Kentucky. Writing after the war, Murray described his first experience camping in the field.

Most of the regiment got to our camp grounds. After stacking our guns, we threw ourselves on the ground with our blankets over us and took what sleep and rest we could. I opened my eyes about sunrise and sat up. Such a night I never dreamed of. There were about 1,000 men scattered over an old trodden camp ground. Not a spear of grass was to be seen. Every man was covered with a blanket or rubber. The bugle sounded and it was not long before all were stirring. . . .

Well we had to get something to eat. After each one had his fire going, we boiled our coffee in a tin cup and ate our hard tack and a slice of raw pork. We were filled and refreshed. Next we pitched our tents. They was what they called the Sibley tent, quite large and oval and open at either end. A pole sat upright, about eight feet high and another across the top. The canvas stretched over the sides and was pegged down to the ground. It was nice to see a company laid out, all being in exact line. Kitchens were in the rear and the officers' tents in the rear of them. As soon as the tents were up, we had to get brushes instead of brooms and police or sweep the camp all over and carry off the dirt.

CORPORAL CHARLES E. CORT
92D ILLINOIS INFANTRY

Charles Cort poses proudly in his new uniform in a photograph taken just before he joined the 92d Illinois in September 1862. Cort served first as an infantryman; later in the war his regiment received horses and became part of John Wilder's Lightning Brigade, a unit of mounted infantry. In a letter to his family he described the novel new shelter tents—or pup tents—that were being issued to the Federal armies.

Franklin, Tenn. April 24, 1863. . . .
Well we have got our shelter tents and I like them better than I thought I would. Each man has a piece of linen (something like them old pants I use to have) 5 1/2 ft square with buttons and button holes on three sides. two of them are buttoned togather & makes a shelter tent for two men. We can button as many together as you wish. we have four togather and four sleep under it.

We take two sticks about four feet high and sharpen them a little to run through the loop holes, set them on the ground then two stakes on each side and one each end to tie the stay ropes to and you have a shelter tent set up. It is four feet high in the center, 5 1/2 long and wide enough to streach out in. Cant tell wheather they will turn rain or not as it has not rained since we got them.

In 1862 Confederate general P. G. T. Beauregard ordered the adoption of small silk camp flags for his Department of South Carolina, Georgia, and Florida. The flags, miniatures of the Confederacy's first national flag, were used to mark the boundaries of regimental encampments. The number 168 is a catalog number, one of which was applied to all Rebel colors captured by Federal forces and turned in to the War Department.

COLONEL THOMAS L. LIVERMORE

STAFF, MAJOR GENERAL WINFIELD SCOTT HANCOCK

In 1861, at age 17, Livermore left college in Illinois and rushed to Washington, D.C., hoping for an appointment to West Point. There, impatient to get into the war, he joined the 1st New Hampshire. By 1864 Livermore was a major on Hancock's staff. At temporary headquarters near Reams Station, Virginia, Livermore learned the perils imposed by the lack of privacy in a tented encampment.

I put the camp on a gentle slope toward Petersburg, arranging the general's, Colonel Morgan's, and one or two others' tents in a line facing Petersburg, and the rest of us in two wings at right angles with that line, thus forming three sides of a square whose fourth side was open toward the works and was the lowest. By this arrangement my tent was brought in one corner near the general's. We had all got well settled in our new quarters, and I had lain down on my bed after dark, when a dog set up a horrible howling in rear of my tent. Major Bull, who was next to me, sallied out and drove him away, and on coming back put his head in at my tent door to receive my congratulations on his success, and just as he had done so, there resounded through the camp another unearthly howl which I took to be the dog's; and to plague Bull I imitated it as a response to his information, in so loud a voice that my howl, too, rang through the camp. Its echoes had not ceased when General Hancock's voice was heard roaring out to his valet, "Shaw! Shaw! Go find that man; I'll see if I can't sneeze in my own camp! Find him! I'll send him to his regiment!" And close upon this astounding information came Shaw to my tent, which was dangerously near the general's, and ducking much, said, "The general, sir, wants to know, sir, who imitated his sneeze, sir?" Said I, "Shaw, it was a dog out in the rear." He trotted back to the general and told him this,

and it added fuel to the general's wrath, and Shaw was impelled back and said that the general didn't think it was a dog, and wanted to know who it was; but I would not divulge the author of that howl while the general was so angry, and gradually the angry ejaculations of that enraged officer subsided, and at a late hour of the night I went into his tent and said, "General, I have come to explain that noise in the camp." He bristled up and said, "Yes, sir," in a ferocious tone. Said I, "It was not in imitation of you, General." Said he, "I don't know who it was, sir, but I think it was, sir, I think it was"; and he seemed to grow angrier with every word. I closed by saying, "Well, General, the fact is I made that noise; there had been a dog howling in rear of my tent and I imitated him." I don't know what conclusion the general drew as to the similarity between his sneeze and the dog's howl, but he replied, in a milder tone, "Very well, sir"; and I retired, and was in as good a position afterwards as before, for all that I ever knew; in fact, it is just to General Hancock to say that he not only never seemed to recollect it afterwards, but distinguished me with more than one great favor.

PRIVATE JOHN W. STEVENS

5TH TEXAS INFANTRY

As a member of John Bell Hood's Texas Brigade, Stevens fought in most of the major campaigns in Virginia until his capture at Gettysburg. Exchanged for medical reasons, he returned home to Texas on furlough in December 1864. After the war Stevens served several terms as a judge in his home state. Here he describes the construction of a soldier's "dog house."

We at once begin to make ourselves as comfortable as possible, each company dividing up into messes. These messes are usually composed of from four to six men. We begin at once to erect our little dog houses. Now as I have promised to tell my young readers about the dog house, I guess I had as well do so here.

We select a tree about ten or twelve inches in diameter, being careful to get one with long straight body, and that has the appearance of splitting well. We cut it up into cuts seven to ten feet long, according to the size of the dog house we want, which is governed by the number of men in the mess. We split the cuts up into slabs about eight inches

Men of the 1st Connecticut Heavy Artillery build winter quarters near Brandy Station, Virginia, in 1864. Most of the log huts had tent canvas roofs, but a few more-elaborate shelters, such as the one next to the photographer's wagon (lower right), were built with planks taken from nearby farm buildings.

thick; then we begin somewhat as you would to build a pig pen, build-ing up one end (to the north) and the two sides, leaving the south end open. We build up about three feet high, then we set up a fork or post at the center of each end, and put a pole across for a ridge pole, or comb of the structure, and over this we place a covering of any thing we can get—usually an old piece of tent cloth, drawing it tightly down to the logs or slabs on each side as tight as we can and making it fast. Then we close up the opening at the north end and close all the cracks, making it

wind tight. We then rake up dry leaves and fill the dog house about ten inches deep with the leaves, which makes us a good warm bed. On these leaves we spread one blanket and use the remainder of our blan-kets for covering. Our fire is built at the open end, the reflection of the heat from the fire striking the top of the covering of this dog house obliquely, is thrown by reflection down upon our bedding, making it quite warm and comfortable. We keep our fires in cold weather all day and pretty well all night.

On Hilton Head Island, South Carolina, men of the 3d New Hampshire Infantry relax in camp around a makeshift table littered with letters, dominoes, an inkwell, and photos from home. While one soldier writes a letter, a companion reads the latest edition of Harper's Weekly. The men sport distinctive "camp caps," off-duty headgear in the form of homemade knit tam-o'-shanters. The colorful example at left was worn by a soldier in the 1st Rhode Island Infantry.

LIEUTENANT LEMUEL P. JEFFRIES
4TH OHIO INFANTRY

In 1861, 22-year-old Lemuel Jeffries left Wooster, Ohio, and the editorship of the Wayne County Democrat to volunteer for the army. He fought with the 4th Ohio at Chancellorsville, Gettysburg, in the Wilderness campaign, and at Cold Harbor. His regiment was even dispatched to New York City to suppress the draft riot in July 1863. Writing in his diary in January of that year, Jeffries described the 4th Ohio's winter camp at Falmouth, Virginia.

January 1, 1863: Falmouth, Va. opposite Fredericksburg. . . .
The huts for winter quarters are of all sizes and designs—some are Indian wigwam style, Irish shanty, Dutch cow barn, Yankee woodshed, &c. The roofs are mainly of the dirty brown "sheltertent" muslin and the chimneys of sticks crossed-mortared together with the *red* clay of this region. The huts are generally from 20 to 30 feet in size. They are dark, dirty and dismal, and cheerless, often full of smoke. Sometimes a chimney would take fire and then there would be a hul-a-baloo! Very disagreeable when smoke, rain and darkness filled the place and men lay cuddled up close shaking and shivering until morning.

PRIVATE THOMAS G. ODELL
78TH ILLINOIS INFANTRY

Thomas Odell, a 31-year-old teacher from Adams County, Illinois, was so inspired by patriotic fervor that he left four children and a pregnant wife to join the 78th Illinois Volunteers. While in the service Odell encouraged his nine-year-old daughter, Mary, to write to him, and he replied with letters that satisfied her curiosity about army life. Odell was severely wounded at Chickamauga in 1863 and spent the remainder of the war in army hospitals.

Fort Joseph on Finger Creek
Nelson County, Ky.
Nov. the 19th/62
Daughter Mary,
. . . I promised Mother I would tell you how our F[ort] is made. It is forty five feet square, one side being a triangle. There are 5 corners to it in each corner, there is a small round house, 15 feet across, the Capt.

"Sometimes a chimney would take fire and then there would be a hul-a-baloo!"

and Lieuts. stay in one of these houses while the men are divided into 4 messes, 23 men in a mess, each mess stays in one of these houses. The fort is all made of round timber set on end, some 10 feet high with portholes for us to shoot through. There is a door to each house and one to the fort. A tent is placed on top of each house to cover it. The ground is our floor, there is some straw on the floor. Two men sleep together. Uncle Risdon and I sleep together, we spread one blanket down on the straw to sleep on, and cover with the other and sometimes we button our overcoats together and spread them over us. We use our knapsack for pillows. Each of us has a wooden pin drove in the logs above our heads on which we hang our guns and other things. You want to know how we make our coffee. Well, we cook out doors altogether as yet, we have a small ditch, or trench, in the ground, the sides of which are fixed up with rock, and a little chimney for the smoke to pass through. We put water in a tin boiler (which holds about as much as our wooden bucket). But I was too fast, we make the fire first, then put on the pot and when it boils we put the coffee in & let it boil five or ten minutes. But I expect you would laugh at our coffee mill were you to see it. George (the darkey who cooks for our mess, I told you about him in my other letter), puts some coffee in a sheet iron pan, which holds about two gallons, sets it on the ground, takes a gun and pounds it till it is fine enough for use. We have a broad plank fixed up for a table, we stand up to eat. Each of us has a tin pan for a plate, a tin cup to drink coffee out of, also a knife, fork and spoon. I believe I told you what we have to eat in my other letter. As to the washing, some of us hire others to wash and others wash for themselves. For my part I do my own washing. Sew on all the buttons that come off, and so on. . . . Take good care of that sweet little sister till I come home. I suppose her name is Elizabeth. Tell Mother to call her Elizabeth Ann.
Your Father,
T. G. Odell

"Some of our boys are not over and above clean and if not pretty sharply looked after would not wash themselves from weeks end to weeks end."

CORPORAL GEORGE H. CADMAN
39TH OHIO INFANTRY

In 1862, five years after leaving England to settle in Ohio, Cadman joined the 39th Ohio Infantry. Promoted to corporal a year later, he described his new rank as "being everyone's dog and nobody's boss." Nevertheless he took pride in his unit, boasting to his wife, Esther, that the 39th was "the Hardest Regt. in the Brigade." Cadman died in 1864, possibly from sunstroke.

Some of our boys are not over and above clean and if not pretty sharply looked after would not wash themselves from weeks end to weeks end. There are two brothers who are especially dirty and if they are left alone for a few days they get such a coat of dirt upon their faces it is impossible to tell one from the other. They would be eaten alive by vermin if it were not for their messmates cursing them. The other day they were both sent down to the creek under the charge of a corporal and two men were detailed to wash them. But I do not think they have washed since and today I saw the Captain giving them the devil again.

Men of Company F of the 22d Connecticut Infantry take a break outside their log cabin in the regiment's quarters at Miner's Hill, Virginia, during the winter of 1862–1863. Their rough but sturdy cabin, complete with a glass window, was fronted by a "corduroy," or log sidewalk, that stretched the length of the street.

"Better be keerful of them ere lice !"

PRIVATE RANDOLPH A. SHOTWELL
8TH VIRGINIA INFANTRY

Shortly after joining his regiment at its winter camp near Centreville in 1861, Shotwell recalled his first spell of duty on the picket lines. Sent to the lines on Christmas Day, the fastidious Shotwell endured a long march in freezing temperatures, only to discover that the picket shelter he was to occupy was infested with lice.

After a weary march of nine miles, the bivouac of the main reserve post was reached; and here we witnessed the first real rejoicing of this Christmas holiday—the joy of the men on duty to be relieved, and allowed to return to camp! Our loss was their gain; and in gratitude they shouted as they gave up their places a very necessary warning. It was couched in three words. "Better be keerful of them ere lice!" In explanation it will be only necessary to state that the rush huts, or "shelters," (made by leaning long saplings, or poles against a tree, or resting them upon a transverse pole between two trees, and covering the poles with boughs, leaves, etc.) had been occupied for months by all kinds of men, including of course, many dirty, slovenly fellows, careless of cleanliness, and dropping vermin wherever they went, to say nothing of where they stretched their dirty blankets. Hence these outpost bivouacs became literally swarming with the hateful insects, and even the greatest care seemed inadequate to prevent their getting a lodgment somewhere in one's clothes or blankets. And once "entrenched" in the seam of a garment, there is no dislodging them as even two hours boiling in hot water merely makes them more vigorous and lively. To escape this "plague of Egypt"... I declined to take possession of any of the deserted quarters, but spent the long night wrapped in my blanket, crouching by the side of the fire in the driving storm. Indeed throughout the entire war, after accustoming myself to coarse, dirty clothing, coarse, dirty food, and coarse, dirty companionship, I could not conquer my intense abhorrence of the pestiferous pests—the "Greybacks." And when upon a long march, with no chance to either obtain a change of underclothing, or wash those I wore, the mortification of knowing the vile vermin were "in possession" and multiplying ten times faster than they could be destroyed, was so great as to make me perfectly *miserable;* so much so that I could think of nothing else.

Leslie's Illustrated artist Edwin Forbes sketched several examples of chimney construction in a winter camp near Falmouth, Virginia. The men in the foreground use fieldstone, while the crew in the background make do with a construction of sticks daubed with mud. A third example in the background employs empty pork or beef barrels. Such expedients often caught on fire, causing, in the words of veteran John Billings, "a lively hurrah to run through the camp."

PRIVATE JOHN D. BILLINGS

10TH BATTERY, MASSACHUSETTS LIGHT ARTILLERY

In civilian life the louse was considered a symptom of poverty and poor morals, but in the crowded and unhygienic armies of the Civil War the tiny parasitic insect made no social distinctions. Veteran artilleryman John Billings recalled with humor the secretive behavior of green soldiers who did not yet realize that everyone shared the ubiquitous graybacks.

Captain John K. Booton of the 11th Virginia Infantry preserved the straight razor that he carried during the war. Many soldiers chose to tolerate the difficulties of shaving in the field rather than grow a beard. The harsh homemade Confederate soap (top) was a welcome gift from loved ones.

The secretiveness which a man suddenly developed when he found himself *inhabited* for the first time was very entertaining. He would cuddle all knowledge of it as closely as the old Forty-Niners did the hiding-place of their bag of gold-dust. Perhaps he would find only *one* of the vermin. This he would secretly murder, keeping all knowledge of it from his tent-mates, while he nourished the hope that it was the Robinson Crusoe of its race cast away on a strange shore with none of its kind at hand to cheer its loneliness. Alas, vain delusion! In ninety-nine cases out of a hundred this solitary *pediculus* would prove to be the advance guard of generations yet to come. . . .

The feeling of intense disgust aroused by the first contact with these creepers soon gave way to hardened indifference, as a soldier realized the utter impossibility of keeping free of them, and the privacy with which he carried on his first "skirmishing," as this "search for happiness" came to be called, was soon abandoned, and the warfare carried on more openly.

In this Edwin Forbes drawing a soldier relaxes in a make-shift chair while the camp barber applies a razor to his whiskers and potential customers look on. "Whether from lack of skill in the use or care of the razor, or from want of inclination," observed John Billings, "a large number preferred to patronize the camp barber" rather than shave themselves.

The haversack, with its liner easily removed for washing (top), was intended to carry rations and eating utensils. This example, which belonged to Private William T. Peyton of the 5th Virginia Infantry, a Federal regiment raised in western Virginia, was made of painted canvas.

PRIVATE WILLIAM BIRCHER

2D Minnesota Veteran Volunteer Infantry

William Bircher and his father, Ulrich, joined the 2d Minnesota in August of 1861 and served together throughout the war. Ulrich did duty as a teamster, while 15-year-old William served as a drummer. After the war the younger Bircher (left) returned to Saint Paul, kept a saloon, and played a drum in the local Great Western Band. He died in 1917 in Florida while serving as mayor of the town of Saint Cloud.

Of provisions Uncle Sam usually gave us a sufficiency, but the table had little variety and fewer delicacies. On first entering the service the drawing of our rations was not a small undertaking, for there were nearly a hundred of us in the company, and it took a considerable weight of bread and pork to feed a hundred hungry stomachs. But after we had been in the field a year or two the call, "Fall in for your hard-tack!" was leisurely responded to by only about a dozen men,—lean, sinewy, hungry-looking fellows, each with his haversack in hand. They would squat around a gum blanket, spread on the ground, on which was a small heap of sugar, another of coffee, another of rice, maybe, which the corporal was dealing out by successive spoonfuls. They held open their little black bags to receive their portion, while near by lay a small piece of pork or beef, or possibly a small amount of desiccated vegetables. Much depended, of course, on the cooking of the provisions furnished us. At first we tried a company cook, but we soon learned the saying of Miles Stan-

dish,—"If you wish a thing to be done well you must do it yourself; if not, you must leave it to others." This applies to cooking quite as well as to courting. We, therefore, soon dispensed with our cook, although scarcely any of us knew how to cook as much as a cup of coffee. When we took the field, a keen appetite, aided by that "necessity" which is ever the mother of invention, soon taught us how to make bean soup and hard-tack,—prepared "hard-tack." It is a question I have much debated with myself, while writing this diary, whether this chapter should not be entitled "hard-tack," as this article of diet was the grand staff of life to the boys in blue. It would seem that but little could be said of the culinary art in camp without involving some mention of hard-tack at almost every turn. If you take a hard-tack in your hand, you will find it somewhat heavier than an ordinary biscuit, but if you will reduce it to a find powder you will find that it will absorb considerably more water than an equal weight of wheat flour; showing that in making hard-tack the chief object in view was to stow away the greatest amount of nourishment in the smallest amount of space. I also observed that hard-tack was very hard. This I attributed to its great age, for there was a common belief among the boys that our hard-tack had been baked long before the beginning of the Christian era. This opinion was based upon the fact that the letters "B.C." were stamped on many, if not, indeed, all the cracker-boxes. To be sure, there were some wiseacres who shook their heads and maintained that these mysterious letters were the initials of the name of some army contractor or inspector of supplies; but the belief was widespread and deep-seated that they were without a doubt intended to set forth the era in which our bread had been baked.

Our hard-tack was very hard. We could scarcely break them with our teeth. Some we could scarcely fracture with our fist. Still, as I have said, there was an immense amount of nourishment stowed away in them, as we soon discovered when once we had learned the secret of getting at it. It required some

The "mess book" shown here was a record of provisions purchased by two Confederate officers. In both the Federal and Confederate armies, officers received cash allowances to buy food, rather than government rations.

experience and no little hunger to enable one to appreciate hard-tack rightly, and it demanded no small amount of inventive genius to understand how to cook hard-tack as they ought to be cooked. If I remember correctly, in our section of the army we had fifteen different ways of preparing them. In other parts, I understood, they had discovered one or two ways more, but with us fifteen was the limit of the culinary art. When this article of diet was on board, on the march they were usually not cooked at all, but eaten in the raw state. In order, however, to make them somewhat more palatable, a thin slice of nice fat pork was cut down and laid on the cracker, and a spoonful of good brown sugar put on top of the pork, and we had a dish fit for a soldier. Of course, the pork was raw and had just come out of the pickle. When we halted for coffee we sometimes had fricasseed hard-tack, prepared by toasting them before the hot coals, thus making them soft and spongy.

It there was time for frying, we either dropped them into the fat in the dry state and did them brown to a turn, or soaked them in cold water and then fried them, or pounded them to a powder, mixed this with boiled rice, and made griddle-cakes and honey,—minus the honey.

When, as was generally the case on a march, our hard-tack was broken into small pieces in our haversacks, we soaked these in water and fried them in pork fat, stirring well and seasoning with salt and pepper, thus making what was commonly called a "hell-fired stew." But the great triumph of the culinary art in camp, to my mind, was "hard-tack pudding." This was made by placing the biscuit in a stout canvas bag, and pounding bag and contents with a club on a log until the biscuits were reduced to a fine powder; then we added a little wheat flour, if we had it,—the more the better,—and made a stiff dough, which we next rolled out on a cracker-box

lid, like a pie-crust; then we covered this all over with a preparation of stewed dried apples, dropping in here and there a raisin or two just for "Auld Lang Syne's" sake, rolled and wrapped it in a cloth, boiled it for an hour or so, and ate it with wine sauce. The wine was usually omitted and hunger inserted in its stead. Thus we saw what truly vast and unsuspected possibilities resided in this innocent-looking, three and a half inch square hard-tack. Three made a meal and nine were a ration, and this was what fought the battles for the Union.

The army hard-tack had but one rival, and that was the army bean, —a small, white, roundish soup-bean. It was quite innocent-looking, as was its inseparable companion, the hard-tack, and, like it, was possessed of possibilities which the uninitiated would never suspect.

It was not so plastic an edible as the hard-tack; nor susceptible of so wide a range of use, but the one great dish which might be made of it was so pre-eminently excellent that it threw "Hell fired stew" and "Hard-tack pudding" quite into the shade. This was baked beans. No doubt bean-soup is very good, as it is also very common. But, oh, baked beans! I had heard of the dish before, but never had remotely imagined what toothsome delights lurked in the recesses of a camp-kettle of beans, baked after the orthodox, backwoods fashion, until one day Bill Hunter, of K Company, whose home was in the lumber regions, where the dish had no doubt been first invented, said to me, "Come around to our tent

A deep three-legged skillet called a spider was commonly used to bake bread over the coals of a campfire. When the Confederate armies experienced shortages of wheat flour (it was packed in bags such as the one shown here), coarse and gritty cornmeal became the staple.

"We baked our bread on an old broken piece of flat iron that we had picked up among the rubbish of a town near our encampment, and cooked our meat (beef) by holding it to the fire on a stick or ramrod."

LIEUTENANT ALBERT T. GOODLOE
35TH ALABAMA INFANTRY

Cooking utensils were always at a premium in Civil War armies. They were easily stolen, were often abandoned on the march, or just wore out from heavy use, and replacements were not readily available. But, as Lieutenant Goodloe recalled in his memoirs, a scarcity of pots and pans only encouraged the men to test their ingenuity and improvisational skills.

to-morrow morning; we're going to have baked beans for breakfast. If you will walk around to the lower end of our company tent street with me, I will show you how we bake beans up in the country I came from."

It was about three o'clock in the afternoon, and the boys were already busy. They had an enormous camp-kettle about two-thirds full of parboiled beans. Near by they had dug a hole in the ground about three feet square and two deep, in and on top of which a great fire was to be made about dusk, so as to get the hole thoroughly heated and full of red-hot coals by the time tattoo sounded. Into this hole the camp-kettle was then set, with several pounds of fat pork on top of the beans, and securely covered with an inverted mess-pan. It was sunk into the red hot coals, by which it was completely concealed, and was left there all night to bake, one of the camp-guards throwing a log on the fire from time to time to keep matters going.

Early the next morning some one shook me roughly as I lay sleeping soundly in my tent: "Get up, Billy! breakfast is ready. Come to our tent. If you never ate baked beans before, you never ate anything worth eating." I found three or four of the boys seated around the camp-kettle, each with a tin plate on his knee and a spoon in his hand, doing their very best to establish the truth of the old adage, "The proof of the pudding is in the eating." Now it is a far more difficult matter to describe the experience of the palate than of either the eye or the ear, and therefore I shall not attempt to tell how very good baked beans are.

*S*ometimes we were supplied with cooking utensils, and sometimes we were not. For a long time, in some of the stages of the war, we baked our bread on an old broken piece of flat iron that we had picked up among the rubbish of a town near our encampment, and cooked our meat (beef) by holding it to the fire on a stick or ramrod; and not unfrequently we were put to the necessity of baking our bread in the ashes. We usually had some kind of tin, good or indifferent, to make up the dough in, but we sometimes had to use hickory bark peeled off in large pieces for that purpose, and would right often cut out a tray in the top of a log.

Among our cooking utensils mention must be made of the frying pans that we made by bursting open Yankee canteens, which we would hold over the fire by slipping the edge of the half canteen into the split end of a stick, which served as a handle. These canteens were made of two concavo-convex tin plates, fastened together around their edges, and which could easily be blown open by putting a little powder in them and igniting it. We would only thus destroy the canteen as such when it began to leak, for we needed all the canteens we could get for carrying water, and then we would use the side that did not leak for a frying pan. This utensil was especially adapted for making cush in out of our bread when it was too old to be good eating otherwise; and our cush was so palatable at times that we would declare that we were going to live on cush altogether when we got home from the war.

In winter quarters at Camp Quantico near Dumfries, Virginia, in 1861, men of the Texas Brigade perform their individual duties for the photographer: clothes washing, wood cutting, and baking a pone of corn bread in a deep skillet. Their sturdy log cabin has a roof of overlapping shingles and a "requisitioned" glass-paned window, but only a canvas flap shields the doorway.

Union messmates, in bivouac on April 30, 1862, near Chancellorsville, Virginia, were sketched by artist Alfred Waud preparing their rations over an open fire, anticipating a supper of broiled meat and boiled coffee. Cooking meat on a ramrod was a common practice, one strictly forbidden by army regulations.

CORPORAL THOMAS W. MOFFATT
12TH ILLINOIS INFANTRY

After participating in General Sherman's march to the sea, Thomas Moffatt recalled the first issue of proper rations after the capture of Savannah in December 1864. Camped "in the most beautiful park in the city," Moffatt's men built an improvised oven and enjoyed "the first soft bread we had had for about a year."

Here's how they build a bake oven in the army: About fifteen or twenty men get a large log or piece of timber and proceed to the nearest empty brick house and, with their improvised battering ram bust the corner out of it. The bricks are cleaned as well as possible and carried to the site of the oven. The heavy work was done mostly by the colored camp followers of whom there were thousands everywhere. And willing workers they were, too. When the bricks arrived at the camp six posts were erected in the form of a rectangle, their tops about three feet above ground. A frame of joists was mortised on the tops of these posts, the lumber for which was appropriated from a dwelling nearby. A floor was nailed on top of this with nails that came with the lumber. A double layer of bricks was laid on top of the wooden floor. In the meantime carpenters had been constructing a number of semi-circular frames. These were erected on the floor of the oven and when covered with thin siding from the house formed a perfect arch. This was then overlaid with bricks laid in mortar

With pans of dough rising and another batch in the making, army bakers (left) prepare bread for Federal soldiers. By 1864 the Federal government had established central bakeries in Washington, D.C., and in Alexandria and Fort Monroe, Virginia, to supply bread for the troops. Most other rations were still cooked by the individual soldier; in a sketch by Edwin Forbes (above), a lone soldier near Petersburg in 1864 cooks his ration of beef in an improvised skillet.

of blue clay and water. The ends were now filled in leaving a hole for the door, and one for the chimney for which we commandeered the smoke stack from a nearby tannery. Over the hole we put a couple of inches of dry sand. A fire was now built inside the oven and all the interior woodwork burned out. The brick arch held up beautifully.

In the meantime the cook had his sponge prepared and when we had the oven good and hot the soft loaves were put in and by supper time we had all the bread we could eat. Just as fine as could be obtained in any city in America. This was the first soft bread we had had for about a year so you can imagine what a treat it was to the men. Especially to soldiers of whom it is said that ninety percent of their thoughts are about eating.

PRIVATE JOHN T. FREDERICK
10TH OHIO CAVALRY

Frederick joined the 10th Ohio Cavalry in northern Georgia in February 1864 and served in the campaign for Atlanta and the march to the sea. The Army of the Cumberland's hard-riding cavalry regiments traveled light, and in an April 1887 article for the National Tribune Frederick recalled the "capture of a skillet" while his company was camped near Gordon's Gap at the start of the Atlanta campaign.

There were seven of us in our mess—Geo. and Joseph Hankinson, Hector Looker, John Grimm, Chas. and Joseph Elston, and myself. We had no skillet in our mess, and had to depend on other comrades for the loan of one when they had finished cooking. As marching orders would frequently come before we had finished our meal, we were not allowed to enjoy our rations as we would like. This could not last always. So we held a council of war and decided that we must have at least two skillets. The lot fell upon Comrades George Hankinson and Hector Looker to get them.

They made a reconnaissance in force about 9 o'clock p.m., finding the 92d Ill. M't'd Inf. in camp just across the creek a short distance from us. They made the necessary dispositions to attack that veteran regiment. Seeing two skillets carelessly exposed in the camp, Comrade Looker seized one and returned to our mess without accident. Comrade Hankinson attempted to obtain the other. The skillet lay by the head of a sleeping man, whose head was pillowed on his saddle, propped on a rail. This was Comrade Hankinson's chance. He grasped the skillet, but the pan would not come. There was a string tied to the handle, and the other end appeared to have caught fast on something. He gave it a jerk, bringing the rail and saddle from under the sleeper's head, who, suddenly awaking, and seeing his pan about to depart, jumped up, giving a Comanche war-whoop. He started after Hankinson, who dropped the skillet and ran for dear life.

Several of the 92d boys joined the pursuit, shouting at every jump. "Halt, you rascal!" Our comrade was chased within a bend of the creek, which was deep in places. Being unable to get around to another point, he made a desperate spring, alighting in the middle of the stream, and receiving a good ducking. He clambered out on the opposite bank and returned to our mess. His pursuers did not follow him beyond the creek, where they stood and showered curses on his head until he disappeared from their sight.

"In two minutes the whole division was up dancing around in the dark like mad, and frantically waving their arms and shouting 'Hooa! Hooa!'"

PRIVATE F. L. BRAXTON
48TH ILLINOIS INFANTRY

Decades after the war, newspaper editors solicited veterans' accounts of their war service, and many ex-soldiers were happy to oblige. One of these was Braxton, whose "most laughable incident" occurred in 1863 in a camp near the Black River after the fall of Vicksburg. Braxton describes one of the unexpected perils of maintaining large herds of beef cattle with the army, for providing fresh meat rations.

We went into camp on a heavily timbered ridge just west of the river. Of course, everybody was tired and worn out, hungry and cross. The weather was very warm, and the men lay down where they stacked arms, without supper or bed, many of them so worried and fatigued that they were sound asleep in a few minutes. The old soldier will remember that occasionally, to supply the army with lean, fresh beef and soup bones, each corps, and sometimes each division, had a herd of poor, lean, lank cattle with them that was driven along with the command, and a number of them slaughtered each night for use next day. Our division had at that time 100 or 150 head of these cattle corraled to the left of the division, and, as before stated, our brigade was lying around promiscuously, some doubly and some in squads, and nearly all sleeping soundly.

Along about 10 or 11 o'clock some "Hoosier" or "Sucker" away up at the left of the division, where the stock was corraled, began to yell "Hooa! Hooa! Hooa!" and in one minute there was a thousand men up hallooing at the top of their voices "Hooa! Hooa!" and in two minutes the whole division was up dancing around in the dark like mad,

and frantically waving their arms and shouting "Hooa! Hooa!" Everybody supposed the cattle had stampeded and were running through the division from left to right, and as everybody was half asleep when they got on their feet, from the hub-bub supposed the cattle to be right on them. It was very dark and hard to distinguish a bellowing bull from a yelling soldier. Some men in their frenzy tried to climb the first tree or sapling they could find. Col. Sanford, of the 48th Ill., upon retiring for the night, had partially disrobed, as many of the other officers of the regiment had done, and stretched himself on the ground at the roots of a large poplar tree. In the midst of the confusion and uproar he was making futile efforts to climb to the first limb of the big tree, some 25 or 30 feet over his head.

Capt. F. M. Galbraith, of Co. I, same regiment, was making desperate efforts to climb a small dogwood bush that would not support his weight. Every time he got up out of supposed harm's way the sapling would bend and let him down to the ground again, and then with a yell, "Hooa! Hooa!" he would spring for the top of the dogwood again. To complicate things a little more, and add to the Captain's downfall, Ike Dobbs was trying to get to the top of the same dogwood at the same time. Everybody was running into everybody, and for a few minutes Capt. Webster, of Co. K, was performing a war dance at the head of his company, with his haversack and canteen swinging above his head as a Comanche would brandish a war club or scalping-knife.

After the excitement was over, the battle fought and the boys were inquiring "Where am I," Col. Sanford, a portly man, was found sitting on the ground with his arms and legs extended around and trying to encircle the poplar tree, thinking he had succeeded in climbing 10 or 15 feet and was safe.

Artist Alfred Waud sketched butchers of the Commissary Department in action, issuing rations of beef to camp orderlies at the headquarters of the Army of the Potomac. Waud's drawing was probably made in March 1863 at Falmouth, Virginia.

With an oversize handle and a flat, rimmed lid that held hot coals, Dutch ovens were necessities for baking cornbread, the staple of the Confederate armies. The Rebels of the Army of Northern Virginia took pains to carry these utensils on campaign; one Federal soldier recalled seeing the woods around Appomattox filled with abandoned ovens. This example was left in one of Stonewall Jackson's camps near Chantilly, Virginia, in September 1862.

LIEUTENANT COLONEL THEODORE LYMAN
STAFF, MAJOR GENERAL GEORGE G. MEADE

Few soldiers had the opportunity to partake of lavish dinner parties such as the one described here by Lieutenant Colonel Lyman in a letter to his wife, Elizabeth. Officers, particularly those who were attached to a general's staff, enjoyed higher pay and easy access to shipping, and they could afford luxuries denied to less affluent enlisted men.

Headquarters Army of Potomac
February 12, 1864
In this epistle I shall describe to you the whirl of fashion, the galaxy of female beauty, the grouping of manly grace. Behold, I have plunged into the wild dissipation of a military dinner-party. The day before yesterday, there appeared a mysterious orderly, with a missive from Colonel Hayes (my classmate) saying that he should next day entertain a select circle at dinner at five of the clock, and wouldn't I come and stay over night. To which I returned answer that I should give myself that pleasure. The gallant Colonel, who commands the 3d Brigade, 1st Division, 5th Corps, has his Headquarters on the north side of the river, about half a mile from Rappahannock station. At 4 P.M. I was ready, very lovely to look on, with full tog and sash, neatly finished by white cotton gloves and my thick laced shoes. With great slowness did I wend on my sable mare, for fear of splashing myself in a run or a puddle. On the other side of the pontoon bridge I fell in with Lieutenant Appleton wending the same way—he splashed his trousers in Tin Pot Run, poor boy! The quarters were not far, and were elegantly surrounded by a hedge of evergreen, and with a triumphal arch from which did float the Brigade flag. Friend Hayes has an elegant log hut, papered with real wall-paper, and having the roof ornamented with a large garrison flag. The fireplace presented a beautiful arch, which puzzled me a good deal, till I found it was made by taking an old iron cogwheel, found at the mill on the river, and cutting the same in two. Already the punctual General Sykes, Commander of the Corps, was there, with Mrs. S., a very nice lady, in quite a blue silk dress. . . . Also several other officers' wives, of sundry ages, and in various dresses. Then we marched in and took our seats, I near the head and between Mrs. Lieutenant Snyder and Mrs. Dr. Holbrook. Next on the left was General Bartlett, in high boots and brass spurs. There must have been

Private William Lowrey (top) of Company F, 10th Ohio Cavalry, saved his smoke-blackened coffee boiler, made from a tin cup, as a memento of the hard-fought campaigns of Chickamauga, Atlanta, and General Sherman's march to the sea. The soldiers supplied their own cups for boiling and drinking coffee.

In this 1861 Alfred Waud drawing, officers of the 3d Brigade, Army of the Potomac, celebrate Thanksgiving with a feast under bowers of pine branches. The artist recorded pots stewing on a camp stove, the warming bonfire, and the dark-colored, familiarly shaped bottles under the dining table.

Thanksgiving in Camp sketched Thursday 28th 1861

some twenty-four persons, in all. The table ran the length of two hospital tents, ingeniously floored with spare boards from the pontoon-train and ornamented with flags and greens. The chandeliers were ingeniously composed of bayonets, and all was very military. Oyster soup had we; fish, biled mutting, roast beef, roast turkey, pies, and nuts and raisins; while the band did play outside. General Sykes, usually exceeding stern, became very gracious and deigned to laugh, when one of his captains said: "He was the mildest-mannered man that ever cut a throat or scuttled ship."

After dinner, songs were encouraged, and General Sykes told two of his Staff, if they didn't sing immediately, he would send them home at once! I sang two comic songs, with immense success, and all was festive. I passed the night there, and took breakfast this morning, when Albert came down with the horses.

SERGEANT MAJOR WILLIAM P. CHAMBERS
46TH MISSISSIPPI INFANTRY

Fervently believing in the South's right to self-government, Chambers quit his job as a teacher and joined one of five state militia companies later combined into the 46th Mississippi. In besieged Vicksburg, in mid-1863, dwindling rations forced Chambers and others defending the city to subsist on rations of army mule. After the war Chambers resumed teaching, married Sarah Ann Robertson, and raised two daughters.

When the siege began we were receiving one-third of a ration of meat and about two-thirds of a ration of meal. This was soon greatly reduced. In lieu of the cornmeal we had cow peas ground and made into bread. This bread after being baked was about the color of an Indian, and a few hours after being baked would, on being broken, show a substance resembling spider webs which would stretch a foot or more before finally breaking. For a time we had fresh beef instead of bacon, and for a few days at one time we had rice bread issued to us. Then the bread ceased altogether. Our ration then consisted of about one teacup-full of boiled peas and a small bit, perhaps about two ounces, of bacon. For several days before the capitulation we had, instead of the bacon, about 3 or 4 ounces of *mule meat.*

Curl the lip in derision if ye will, ye dainty epicures, but I ween ye never tasted a morsel more sweet than *"mule meat and peas"* was to us! The flesh of the mule seemed of coarser grain, but more tender than that of the ox, and had a decidedly "horsey" flavor. To starving men, however, it was very good. I have strong reason to believe that a dog had been eaten in a Louisiana regiment a long time before any mule beef was issued to us, and I know that a mule killed near our line the first week of the siege was partly cut up and presumably eaten by some of our men. And as to the peas! I have wondered while eating them if I would ever again find anything else that tasted so well.

LIEUTENANT ALBERT T. GOODLOE
35TH ALABAMA INFANTRY

By the beginning of 1862 the South had run out of coffee, and the increasingly effective Federal blockade of Southern ports ensured that no fresh supplies would be arriving. For the coffee-mad Confederate troops it was a crisis that called for a creative bent. As Goodloe tells us in his memoirs, the men invented all sorts of substitute brews, using whatever was available.

It was extremely seldom that genuine coffee was seen in the South anywhere at that time, and the housekeepers in every direction had fallen upon various expedients to furnish themselves with coffee substitutes, which went by the name of coffee. Parched rye, ground and boiled, came into more general use than any other substitute. Parched wheat was also used a good deal, and had a much more pleasant odor than the rye "coffee" had. Sweet potato "coffee" came into use after the others did, and became quite popular. They were cut up into little pieces about the size of a grain of corn and dried in the sun. These pieces were then parched and ground, and otherwise prepared as coffee is. This was a very pleasant beverage, and had rather more the appearance of good coffee than the others did. In the army we made our coffee out of parched meal mainly. At Port Hudson we tried parched sugar, which was the best of all substitutes that I had ever seen; the color and odor and flavor resembling coffee in a surprising manner. Of course we dropped this substitute when we left the sugar region.

"Curl the lip in derision if ye will, ye dainty epicures, but I ween ye never tasted a morsel more sweet than *'mule meat and peas.'*"

COLONEL JAMES COOPER NISBET

66TH GEORGIA INFANTRY

The story offered below from Nisbet's memoirs, Four Years on the Firing Line, *is an apocryphal tale that circulated during the evacuation of Atlanta in 1864. The story stresses the very real problem of the food shortages Confederate soldiers were facing during the siege of the city.*

Unlike their foe, soldiers of the Union armies enjoyed a steady supply of coffee throughout the war. According to the label attached to the bag, this ration of beans was drawn by William Peyton of the Federal 5th Virginia Infantry in camp at Culpeper, Virginia, on August 19, 1862.

We passed down Peachtree Street on our way to join Walker's Division on the McDonough road. Sherman was shelling the city. The fine residences had been hastily abandoned, the owners leaving their lares et penates behind in their hasty flight. We were resting, the men lying about on the streets and sidewalks. One of the men, a tall, lanky "rube," was stalking up and down the sidewalk, oblivious to bursting shells, eating hard-tack. A voice from one of the trees said: "Give poor Polly a cracker!" The country youth stopped, and looked around. Again, "Give poor Polly a cracker," came from the tree. Finally he spied the parrot and said: "Gee Whilkens, boys, damned if the world hain't coming to an end! Even the birds are talking and begging for bread." Looking up he addressed the parrot: "Sure you are a mighty smart bird, and I'm sorry for you, but you go to hell! This is the first cracker I've seen for two days!"

CORPORAL TALIAFERRO N. SIMPSON
3D SOUTH CAROLINA INFANTRY

Once the armies settled down in their winter camps, freight wagons bearing boxes from home began to arrive. Corporal Tally Simpson's effusive letter to his Aunt Caroline expressed his heartfelt joy at receiving such largess. Food and clothing from home provided an important supplement for Confederate soldiers, who faced chronic shortages of nearly all essentials.

Camp near Fredericksburg
Jan 22nd /63
My very dear Aunt. . . .
Ere this reaches you, you will have heard of the reception of that glorious box of good things. Never in my life have I enjoyed good things from home (I call your house my home as well as Mt Jolly) to more entire satisfaction. Tis useless to enumerate the many delicious articles contained in it, but suffice it to say that I have been eating, eating, eating, and am still eating, and some still remain. Oh! how I made "them sassengers and that old ham" howl! "Old Miller" and the rest, tho doing full justice to things in general, could not repress a smile at the savage ferocity with which I made a simultaneous attack upon the whole box. To say that I thought of you all many times while making the desperate charge would be superfluous, for what ungrateful wretch could tickle his appetite with such a delightful repast and be unmindful of the kind ones who troubled themselves for his unworthy sake? No, I am not such an ingrate. A thousand thanks, my dear Aunt, for such an abundance of delicacies.

Having consumed all but the fruit, we have been feasting upon excellent blackberry and peach pies. But alas! even this last resort is almost gone, only two more dinners on pies and the "jig" is up. And we will only live in anticipation of a better time to come. I can never forget you for such kindness. I know Carrie and Ressie had some thing to do in filling the box. Kiss them sweetly for me, and tell them I love them very much. I will write to them the first opportunity without waiting upon them any longer.

SERGEANT WILLIAM J. REICHARD
128TH PENNSYLVANIA INFANTRY

Reichard served with o the 128th Pennsylvania for nine months before mustering out in May 1863. But just before the Battle of Gettysburg, he responded to the call for volunteers to defend the state and rejoined—this time as a sergeant in the 41st Pennsylvania. When the Rebel threat to Pennsylvania ended he was discharged after 34 days. While camped with the 128th at Maryland Heights near Harpers Ferry in October 1862, he received a box from home.

Now for the box, the bread is good it was outside a little mouldy, but cut it off. The doughnuts were most all spoiled anything baked in fat wont keep I have found out and aint healthy for us. The little round sugar cakes were a little spoiled from the doughnuts but can use most all. The rusks were nice the 2 sugar cakes are nice only got a little wet dont hurt them. The sponge cake is pretty nice yet. The butter, jellies, & catsup are bunkin, the other jar of jelly I have not opened yet, until the one is empty especially as Wilgh. has some also, but he cant come up with my butter. The [apples] are very nice I will save them a while if I can. I would like to mention all the things but cant bring them to mind just now. That inkstand came very handy but am sorry to say that my pen came away and is no where to be found, so I borrow one. Ellen the box, is safe, the rebels did not get it have no alarm about it, sleep well on it, Ha Ha. I will write to Eddie pretty soon, if there are any other I have not written to I must have forgot it so they must excuse me. My health is recovering fast since I have the medicine and teas. I am too thankful for them I dont drink any coffee so you can send such teas often in papers if only a little at a time. The bologna sausages are nice but I can not eat much, dry beef would have been better. Wilgh. has been sick for the last 2 days but I hope he may soon be right again. It is cold & windy today, but pretty warm in our tent. Milt returned with the pickets to camp yesterday noon. He was quite surprised to see such a pile of boxes he thought that we might call it an express office.

FA 655

HARPER'S WEEKLY.

A JOURNAL OF CIVILIZATION.

VOL. VI.—No. 262.] NEW YORK, SATURDAY, JANUARY 4, 1862. [SINGLE COPIES SIX CENTS. $2 50 PER YEAR IN ADVANCE.

Entered according to Act of Congress, in the Year 1861, by Harper & Brothers, in the Clerk's Office of the District Court for the Southern District of New York.

Christmas Boxes in Camp—Christmas, 1861.

Agents of this Company are instructed not to forward this without its being Sealed as directed. S. M. SHOEMAKER, Sup't.

Forwarded by the Adams Express Company.

HATTERAS INLET, N.C.   SOLDIER'S PACKAGE.

$ 50 00/100 Enclosed.

For *Dr. H. Pleasants*

FROM *Capt. H. Pleasants*   *Philadelphia*
New Berne, N.C.   *Pennsylvania*

This Adams Express Company "money order," shown above with its wax-sealed reverse, was wired from New Bern, North Carolina, by Captain Henry Pleasants, of the 48th Pennsylvania, to his father, Dr. H. Pleasants, in Philadelphia. In addition to reliable money orders, the Adams Express Company transported "express boxes," filled with items ranging from luxuries to necessities, to soldiers in the field. The arrival of such boxes in camp was greeted with much enthusiasm, as illustrated by Winslow Homer on the front page of the January 4, 1862, issue of Harper's Weekly.

"We sold at $2.00 a piece at camps, upon an average of five hundred to eight hundred per week, so you see we turned a nice penny on ginger cakes."

PRIVATE ROBERT A. JARMAN
27TH MISSISSIPPI INFANTRY

Leaving his family plantation in Monroe County, 21-year-old Robert Jarman joined the 27th Mississippi in September 1861. His father was killed in a Federal raid in 1864 and Jarman returned at war's end to manage the estate. Marrying late in life, Jarman had only nine years to devote to a wife and two daughters before he was killed in a railroad accident in 1893.

Those of us who had servants and a little money began to write passes for them and send them down into Georgia to get something extra for us to eat, and to sell to others. I sent Rafe and Mr. Peck sent his boy, Henry. Rafe brought back potatoes, flour, and molasses, but Henry brought ginger cakes from Big Shanty, near Marietta. Ginger cakes sold like "hot cakes" and that settled the question as to what it would pay to buy. Mr. Peck about this time happening upon a recruit got a forty days furlough to go home. So Jim Thompson and myself fell heir to his ginger cake trade and kept it up all winter, buying at Big Shanty where they were baked especially for us at $1.00 each for about the size of an ordinary plate and one inch thick; we sold at $2.00 a piece at camps, upon an average of five hundred to eight hundred per week, so you see we turned a nice penny on ginger cakes, and it enabled us to get for our mess many extras that winter. Besides, Rafe brought back nearly every trip for us a bottle of apple or peach brandy and he made upon an average two trips a week, and sometimes three.

Faced with a choice, Federal soldiers browse through a cluster of sutlers' establishments at City Point, near Petersburg, Virginia, in early 1865. Whether from a tent, horse-drawn wagon, or more permanent structure, government-licensed vendors—or sutlers—catered to every whim, offering goods such as oysters, tobacco, cakes and pies, boots, or tailored uniforms.

Recovered from a house in Fredericksburg, Virginia, this sardine can was probably left by a Union soldier on picket duty. Commonly sold by sutlers, imported sardines were a popular delicacy that most soldiers could afford.

Sutlers provided easy credit to cash-strapped soldiers. A soldier could simply sign a pay voucher (top right) that allowed the sutler to collect directly from the pay-master on payday. If the soldier paid cash, he might be given his change in "sut-ler's scrip" (top left and center), redeemable only at the sutler's establishment.

PRIVATE CHARLES F. MCKENNA

155TH PENNSYLVANIA INFANTRY

Trade between soldiers and sutlers tended to be one-sided—in favor of the sut-ler. Since the sutler held a monopoly, he could charge high prices, and many sol-diers were drawn into escalating debt through the sutler's system of credit. In a letter to his brother, McKenna described the system into which he and his mates were inevitably enticed.

Extra provisions are very dear and consequently anyone desiring to indulge in an occasional improvement on Uncle Sam's fare will soon find his pecuniary condition diminishing, if not exhausted like mine at present. Bread about half the size of a brick and near as hard is ten cents a loaf, gingerbread, sugar crackers, cheese, onions, dried beef, Bologna Apples &c are the same in proportion. Yesterday after coming in off picket Jas. O'Niell bought two loaves of bread at the Sutlers—while I bought a half pound of butter from a peddler in camp at 15 cents. The sutler has established a system of credit that I have not availed myself of yet. It is that of having a check from the capt. of our Co. and from the purchaser on the paymaster of the army promising to pay the Sutler so much, one, two or three dollars of the purchasers wages. He will give articles to us if we get those checks. Nearly all the men in camp have obtained these checks; till yesterday I had money and did not need them. I had to buy stockings, handkerchief, paper and papers besides provisions and some small sums I loaned, too small to refuse yet amounting to something altogether; this soon took all the cash I received.

"When the sutler came back and found that his cakes had disapeared, a look of blank astonishment settled on his face."

PRIVATE ALFRED BELLARD
5TH NEW JERSEY INFANTRY

The English-born Bellard enlisted when the carpenter to whom he was apprenticed fled to Canada, afraid the South might take the war straight through New Jersey. His regiment was stationed near Rum Point Landing, Maryland, when he recorded in his diary an incident involving a sutler. An unpopular sutler often became the target of retribution ranging from simple shoplifting to mob action.

Our company being detailed for picket at Rum Point Landing, we had, taking it altogether, a very good time. The mud was very bad being up to our ancles, and tramp, tramp, through this was not very pleasant. But all that was forgotten when the sutler's stores arrived. The boys offered their services to load his waggon which was accepted, and boxes of pies and barrells of cake were taken from the boat and placed in his waggon. There not being room for all of it the rest were placed under the dock (in a safe place as the sutler thought), as a sentinel was pacing his beat close by. The sutler being ready to return to camp, the boys thought it was high time that he forked over, but being offered the large ammount of one pie for about a dozen men, they got rather cranky and made a rush for the waggon intending to upset his apple cart, but his horse was whipped up and his goods saved. The sutler being gone, our attention was taken up with the cakes under the dock, and the way those cakes disapeared was a caution. When the sutler came back and found that his cakes had disapeared, a look of blank astonishment settled on his face, and making his way to the captain's quarters stated his grievances to him. The only satisfaction he got was, that government troops were not there to guard sutlers' stores, but the government's, and if he did not want his things stolen, he must guard them himself.

PRIVATE JACOB W. BARTMESS
39TH INDIANA MOUNTED INFANTRY

A farmer and blacksmith, Bartmess joined the 39th Indiana in late 1862, leaving his family behind in New Corydon, Indiana. Captured after the Battle of Stones River but soon exchanged, he visited the family at home before returning to his regiment in Tennessee. In camp he wrote this letter to his wife, Amanda, describing his successful foraging expeditions.

July 11th. *63.*
Camp at Winchester *Ten.*
Dear Wife—. . . .
We are now in camp at winchester. a little town about four miles in the rear of the camp that I wrote from the other time. It has been 17 days since we left Murfreesboro It has been quite a hard trip. Our supply train just came up to us yesterday evening the first that we have seen of it for nearly two weeks. nearly all that time we have had to live off the country We would go out foreageing as we call it. and where ever we could find any corn we would take it for our horses. and then go in the smokehouses and take hams and shoulders or side meat or any thing that could be found to eat. chickens, geese, turkeys, hogs, and cattle were taken very freely. We had to get corn meal werever we could for bread. I got three plugs of tobacco at Tullahoma each about one foot long. which did me very good service. I traided some of it to the *101st Ohio reg't.* for crackers and in this way kept in something to eat.

There are a great many black berrys here and the largest ones you ever seen. A lot of us went out yesterday and got all that we wanted to eat. and brought some to camp.

Well Amanda you ought to see us go into oats fields and meadows with our horses. I tell you, you would see oats and grain suffer. and wheat fields that have the wheat cut and shocked we go into and carry out the wheat to feed, and make beds to sleep on. I tell you that the country is perfectly ransacked We have stirring news here now. but I expect you have heard it all. The boys are in good spirits, thinking that the war will close this sumer.

Alfred Waud sketched two parties of Federal foragers. In the top drawing, soldiers sit in a cornfield, enjoying a meal of roasted corn-on-the-cob, while their fellows in the lower sketch display the results of a raid on a farmyard. When regulations against foraging were not strictly enforced, most soldiers were inclined to supplement their rations at the expense of local citizens.

PRIVATE W. C. YARD
4TH PENNSYLVANIA CAVALRY

In the October 22, 1896, edition of the National Tribune, W. C. Yard recalled a foraging incident near Fredericksburg on June 1, 1862, that involved milk and honey. The cavalry, according to John Billings in his book, Hardtack and Coffee, had the advantage in foraging; they were advancing ahead of other troops and nothing could "escape the most rigid inspection."

While here the boys of the battalion took several swarms of bees, and, to get all the good out of them they could, it was done at night. A good supply of milk was on hand, and honey, milk, and hardtack was a good ration at the time, but the doctors had a hard time to get some of them to live. We all had the honey-milk sickness.

A tall, lank rebel owner of a crib of corn wanted a "gawd put on the kaun," which the Colonel did, and the boys got so excited about it they fed the corn to Uncle Sam's horses, and what they wouldn't eat they carried and threw into the river. The boys didn't believe in guarding rebel property.

One morning a sleek old rebel came to our camp and requested the Captain to put five of the boys under arrest, whom he pointed out, for drinking milk in his spring-house without permission. He also wanted a guard over the premises. He said "when Gen. Lee was along thaur we-all had no gawd, but you-all steal our things." Ab Schnyler said to the Captain, "For Uncle Sam's sake, let me shoot the top of his head off," at the same time drawing a bead on the old fellow. "I came down here all the way from Pennsylvania to shoot such things as that." But the Captain said, "No, don't," as the old fossil went head over heels toward home.

In Charles Reed's lithograph, two Federal pards amble down a country road after bagging a goose, as a local resident watches from behind a rail fence. The sketch gives no clue as to where these hunters found their prize—roaming free, or pecking at corn in a farmer's barnyard.

MAJOR SILAS T. GRISAMORE
18TH LOUISIANA INFANTRY

In 1861 Grisamore, a 36-year-old merchant, joined the Lafourche Creoles, a company of the 18th Louisiana. His business experience and knowledge of shorthand earned him the position of assistant quartermaster, and in 1864 he rose to the rank of major. The incident of the "jumping hogs" occurred while his regiment was marching along the Red River, en route to Alexandria, Louisiana. In his portrait at left, Grisamore appears in the regalia of an Odd Fellow.

The next morning as we were preparing to move, the rain began to fall slowly, and by ten o'clock it was pouring down in torrents, which continued for three hours. Captain Shepherd had just gotten his train across a muddy bottom when the rain stopped everything and in a short time the Crescent wagons were all standing in water three or four feet deep. . . .

In our train we had one of those rolling monuments of human folly and inhumanity known as a three-mule cart, which stuck in a deep hole. Finding the mules could not pull it out, Capt. Shepherd ordered it to be unloaded, and noticing that the driver was rather slow in his movements, he had to repeat the command, when the first thing that was tumbled out was a fat hog that would have weighed about 200. Nobody knew how it had gotten into the wagon, but "Goss" was connected with that train for that day, and we each formed our own opinions. The general impression was, however, that hogs were good jumpers in that section of the country and that this one had leaped into this cart. At sundown we reached a creek from which the bridge had been carried away after the troops and commissary trains had passed over. The men with the provisions were five miles ahead, and we had the utensils and nothing to cook, but nature often provides

where man fails in that important particular.

As we were getting out some pots to cook up what few things we could scrape together, we found that two more 200 pounders had jumped into another one of our wagons, the effort having been so great as to have cleaned themselves nicely by the operation. Out of this bountiful provisions of jumping hogs, which Nature had grown in these woods, we procured a good supper. Some remarks were overheard by some of the soldiers the next evening, when we reached camp, about the quantity of "grease" they had lost, but whether it had anything to do with our supper of the previous night, I never learned.

PRIVATE A. C. BROWN
2D OHIO INFANTRY

In a letter published in the July 22, 1886, issue of the National Tribune, Brown recalls how a forager took humorous revenge on his commanding officer while his regiment was encamped in Tennessee during the Tullahoma campaign.

We had been marching and skirmishing with Bragg's army for about two weeks, and during this time it had rained 14 days and nights, and the mud was so deep that our cracker train was far behind. Being short of rations, foraging was carried on quite extensively, whole flocks of sheep would disappear as if by magic. The planters complained to "Pap" Thomas, and in order to satisfy them and keep up appearances, Gen. Thomas issued one of his famous orders against foraging. This was intended to soothe the old planter, and was not expected to be put into execution. When near Cowan Station, Tenn., the sun came out for the first time for several days. We called a halt and hung ourselves up to dry.

Jack Derrer, of Co. D, 2d Ohio, a crack forager, started out on a stroll. He soon came to a graveyard; in getting over the fence he discovered that the ground had recently been disturbed and came to the conclusion

"When near Cowan Station, Tenn., the sun came out for the first time for several days. We called a halt and hung ourselves up to dry."

Colonel Benjamin Franklin Scribner, veteran of many campaigns and the butt of the practical joke described in A. C. Brown's account beginning on page 116, was a stickler for discipline. In his memoirs Brown recalled the "dog story," remarking that "the acute sense of the ludicrous . . . can nowhere be more strikingly observed than among the soldiers." But in Scribner's retelling, the victim of the joke was not himself but a fellow officer.

it was not a grave. With a piece of a rail he soon resurrected some nice hams. On his way back to camp and when near Col. Scribner's headquarters (commander of the First Brigade), Derrer was arrested, the meat taken from him, and he was admonished not to forage any more. He was then permitted to go to his company. You may depend that Jack was not in the best frame of mind when he entered camp. Derrer related his grievances to the writer and swore vengeance against Col. Scribner and staff for enforcing Pap Thomas's order and confiscating the ham for their own use. After a consultation it was agreed that Derrer was to try his hand the next morning. So, bright and early, Derrer was on the war path. About a mile from camp Jack killed a large, fat bull-dog, skinned out the hindquarters, cut the shank short, and started for camp. When near headquarters Derrer was arrested, placed under guard, and the

meat confiscated. The dog leg of mutton was soon served up, and after Scribner and staff had dined sumptuously on dog leg-of-mutton soup, and were picking their teeth, the barking commenced in Co. I, 2d Ohio. Little dogs, big dogs, old dogs and young dogs barked and howled, and it was the dog-on'ist time I ever did see. The provost guards were sent over to stop the racket and arrested a Co. I boy. The rest of the company surrounded the guard, and they were glad to make terms for themselves, with the condition that they were to go back to headquarters and have Derrer released, as it was he who had fed the whole capoodle on dog. Jack was released, but the barking did not cease. It seemed to be contagious, and went all through the 2d Ohio, and then the brigade. Afterwards when on the march you could always tell when Scribner was passing the 2d Ohio, as they always saluted him with a bark.

Trussed and skewered, a fat hog roasts over a bonfire while Union soldiers anticipate the feast to come. Two men bring fence rails to feed the blaze, while another (at right) stokes the flames. Alfred Waud sketched these men in their bivouac near Munson's Hill, Virginia, in 1861 not long before the Battle of Bull Run. The artist described the pig as the result of "a successful forage in the enemies' country."

a successful forage in the enemies country, of Mansons hill —

The Promise of Home

Looking back on his wartime experiences, Federal colonel James F. Rusling observed, "Many a patriot who enlisted enthusiastically early in 1861 soon wished himself home again —and wished it eagerly." For thousands of soldiers, Union and Confederate, homesickness proved to be as great a strain as the hardships of the march and the dangers of battle. *The Official Medical History of the Civil War,* compiled by the office of the surgeon general, went so far as to class *nostalgia*—defined as "a morbid degree of home feeling"—as a disease that resulted in the hospitalization of more than 5,200 Federal soldiers. In the case of 30-year-old private Ezra Bingham of the 161st Ohio, "nostalgic influence" was listed as the primary cause of death.

With so many volunteers in their teens, it was only natural that their protracted absence fostered a longing for the security of home. "Mamma I dream about you all nearly every night," wrote 19-year-old Eli Landers of the 16th Georgia Infantry; "Mamma I think about you every hour in the day." Married men worried that their paltry army salary would fail to sustain their loved ones, or that their wives would prove unequal to the physical demands of plowing and harvesting the family farm. "Oh how much trouble and unhappiness I have caused you," Iowa lieutenant Henry Ankeny penned his wife, Fostina; "had I taken your advice and remained at our own peaceful home how much better it would have been."

The morale of men at war could sometimes be sustained if they knew that their families manifested a similar devotion to the cause. "I glory in your patriotism, mother," wrote 95th Illinois sergeant Stephen Rollins, "and I can tell you that your words of comfort and loyal cheer have done me much good." Vermonter Byron Wilson queried his younger sibling, "Now are you as *fully patriotic* as a sister of mine ought to be? Are you not willing to give me up, if it *be my lot* to fall in battle?" Having vowed to see the war through to the

A female visitor sits with staff officers of Captain James M. Robertson's 1st Brigade Horse Artillery in front of a headquarters hut at Brandy Station, Virginia, in February of 1864. Opinions about spousal visits were mixed: One Federal officer remarked, "I think I should consider some time before I brought my wife to a mud-hill."

end, Wilson was one of 84 members of the 4th Vermont who perished in the Battle of the Wilderness.

Absent fathers often attempted to impart their sense of duty and pride of service to children too young to understand the complex issues that had driven the nation to war. Following the Battle of Chancellorsville in May 1863, Union colonel Joshua Lawrence Chamberlain informed his six-year-old daughter, Daisy, that "a great many men were killed or wounded." The former college professor continued, "We shall try it again soon, and see if we cannot make those Rebels behave better, and stop their wicked works in trying to spoil our Country, and making us all so unhappy." The wife and child of Confederate colonel E. Porter Alexander were within earshot of the fight at Chancellorsville. "I was interested afterward to hear that our little 18 months old daughter was greatly excited over it," Alexander recalled, "& made the longest sentence she had yet produced, 'Hear my papa shoot Yankee. Boo!'"

Many women sought an active role in the struggle. They raised funds for the war effort at large patriotic bazaars, traveled to the camps as members of the U.S. Christian and Sanitary Commissions, or served as nurses in crowded military hospitals. Women proved adept at gathering intelligence on enemy strength and troop movements— either from personal observation or from talkative military personnel. A number of the war's most celebrated spies were women, while others risked imprisonment to smuggle medical supplies through the lines.

Some disguised their gender so convincingly that they were accepted as recruits in volunteer regiments. Though most female soldiers were ultimately found out and sent home, a few—such as Rosetta Wakeman of the 153d New York—successfully passed themselves off as young men and served through the war.

The wives of senior officers sometimes proved more effective in obtaining supplies for their husbands' regiments than army quartermasters had been. Mrs. Jane Saunders Johnson, the wife of Confederate colonel Bradley T. Johnson, saw to it that 500 rifles, 10,000 cartridges, and much-needed camp gear was issued to her husband's 1st Maryland Infantry. Impressed by her persuasiveness, one official remarked, "If great events produce great men, great events produce great women." Accompanied by three attractive young female acquaintances, Mrs. Johnson spent the winter in camp, providing an immeasurable boost to the Marylanders' morale. "They cheered and ministered to the sick,"

one officer recalled, "and the charm of their sweet and graceful presence turned gloom into sunshine, and shone like an oasis on the dreariness of camp life."

"I have often thought," wrote Confederate major Silas T. Grisamore, "that the most effectual way of restoring a man's love to his wife when it becomes cool, would be to put him in the army, and in a very short time he would be seeking a furlough." For men denied the presence of female society, the appearance of a woman in camp could create quite a sensation. "The Quartermaster's wife came out to see guard mounting," Lieutenant Charles Haydon of the 2d Michigan noted in the winter of 1862; "I thought the men would go crazy at the sight of her ankles. She is a very pretty lady," Haydon confessed, "& has indeed as pretty a pair of ankles as ever I looked upon."

As the war ground on, the exchanges between soldier and civilian turned increasingly sour. Many on the home front were subjected to the ravages of the contending armies, as thousands of hungry soldiers foraged for food and firewood. The destruction of private property was particularly hard felt in the occupied South, where many Federal commanders came to look upon the dep-

The silk tobacco bag shown at left, carefully crossstitched by Retta Patton of Tennessee for Confederate soldier James B. Coleman, is typical of such pouches sent as tokens of affection to soldiers, particularly in the Southern armies. Many wartime photographs show Confederate soldiers proudly displaying their tobacco pouches looped through the buttonholes of their jackets.

redations as a necessary evil. Orders to spare farmers by taking only the top rail of a fence for firewood became a standing joke among Yankee troops—for the "top rail" was soon on the bottom, whereupon it, too, was carried away to a company's campfire. While some destruction was a matter of survival, at other times it was a case of wanton vandalism. "If there be any in the shape of chairs, tables, carpets, crockery, books, tools, musical instruments, or anything else that we want, we take them," confessed Massachusetts volunteer Roland E. Bowen; "if not, why we just kick them to pieces." Rebel soldiers were not averse to foraging either, even if the victims were fellow Southerners. "The troops not only rob the fields," admitted Surgeon Spencer G. Welch of the 13th South Carolina, "but they go to the houses and insist upon being fed, until they eat up everything about a man's premises which can be eaten."

The tragedy of the Civil War extended beyond the armies in the field and left a legacy of sorrow for generations to come. "My thoughts ask me where are the many little orphans calling and crying for pappy," wrote Jacob Bartmess, who had left his wife and four children to enlist in the 39th Indiana. "O, who will answer for the sin of this most dreadful and calamitous war?"

An unidentified young woman gazes from an ambrotype found in the pocket of a dead Confederate soldier. The nearness of death during the war led to the constant exchange of photographs between home and the front. Images of soldiers were commonly accompanied by the phrase "so that you may remember me."

"You cannot imagine, John, the perfect breakdown that would occur in Southern society if slavery were wiped out."

CHAPLAIN SAMUEL C. BALDRIDGE
11TH MISSOURI (U.S.) INFANTRY

Ordained as a Presbyterian minister in 1854, Baldridge was working in a small parish in Wabash County, Illinois, when he joined the 11th Missouri in July 1862. He was with the unit through the battles at Iuka and Corinth but resigned his commission after just six months, citing frustration with his work and an unspecified "domestic calamity" at home. In this letter to his brother-in-law, the chaplain predicts the demise of Southern society should slavery be abolished.

North Alabama is a "goodly land" & splendidly improved as a general thing. I have never seen such *residences in the country,* any place else. Usually 4 square, embowered in trees with a village of Negro quarters flanking in the background. But there are not many fences now & the fruit, fowls, sheep, swine, everything that the soldiers can swallow, together with horses, mules, Negroes &c are finding their way into the camp. You cannot imagine, John, the perfect breakdown that would occur in Southern society if slavery were wiped out. We have nothing in the North to correspond to the relation of master & slave. The masters would pine & starve . . . until they could learn the arts of honest labor. I am persuaded that so far as the *present Lords* of the soil are concerned, the South is entirely ruined, if this institution goes down, in this fiery storm. The only hope is immigration. The Northerner & the English & the German must come in & supplant & possess or this fine country will remain a desolation when the slaves are gone. But let this incubus be removed & the country be opened & these valleys would soon fill up.

Oxford, Mississippi, lies in ruins after being sacked by Major General Andrew J. Smith's Federal troops in August 1864. Smith's main objective was to capture the Rebel cavalry leader Nathan Bedford Forrest, but when Forrest proved elusive, Smith gave the order to destroy the town. Smith's men—"made mad with whiskey," according to Confederate observers—burned more than 40 homes and businesses, as well as the Oxford courthouse.

Federal soldiers dismantle a fence for firewood in this drawing by Edwin Forbes. Many officers discouraged this practice—it was devastating to a farmer to lose his livestock corral—but men of both sides found such ready supplies of dry, seasoned wood hard to pass up.

2. column

PRIVATE ALFRED BELLARD
5TH NEW JERSEY INFANTRY

By late 1862 Bellard's regiment had fought in the Peninsula campaign and at Second Manassas and was marching through rain and snow toward Fredericksburg. Tired and hungry, the soldiers were in no mood to humor the Virginia shopkeeper mentioned in this journal entry. Bellard later received a leg wound at Chancellorsville and was hospitalized while the 5th New Jersey fought at Gettysburg. By 1881 Bellard's old injury had become so troublesome that he applied for a military pension.

Passing through the town of Dumfries, we went into camp about 8 miles beyond. While we were passing through the town, some of the boys went into a variety store that we passed to purchase some tobacco, but the proprietor said that he had none, and would not sell any for our money, if he had. Some sharp eyed blue coat however spied a barrel of it in the cellar, and on its being noised around a grand rush was made for that barrell. And it was not long before Mr. Reb had none in reality, and with none of our cash for it either. I managed to fill my pockets with it, so that I was fixed. The tobacco question being disposed of, attention was paid to the ballance of his stock in trade. Dry goods were thrown down from the shelves, on to the counter, and were soon converted into gun rags by as many men as could crowd into the store. Ladies' crinoline were strewn around, and in fact everything that was in the store was torn up, carried away, or distroyed, even to his cash box. When the sacking became general, the proprietor got afraid of his life and left to find the Genl. While he was gone the stable was opened, his saddle was brought out and given to one of our officers, who rode off with it. The horse was next trotted out, and would have been trotted out of reach in a few minutes had not the Genl. appeared just as we got him out of the stable, and ordered us to return it. We did so, but that was all he did get back that was of any value. I rather think that when U.S. troops passed his way again he was more obliging and so save his reputation and his goods at the same time.

A detachment of Federal soldiers near Harpers Ferry forages for hay in October 1863. To minimize the destruction of private property that often took place when the men were left to their own devices, many Union commanders organized special foraging details.

LIEUTENANT STEPHEN W. HAYDON
2D MICHIGAN INFANTRY

A lawyer who had studied at the University of Michigan, Stephen Haydon was appalled by the vandalism wrought by his men. In this 1861 entry from his diary he shows particular contempt for those who would desecrate a church. Haydon was seriously wounded at Jackson, Mississippi, in 1863 and fell ill with pneumonia while headed home on furlough in early 1864. He died a few weeks later.

Pohick Church is a brick building built in 1773. Gen. Washington contributed to building it & was a frequent attendant. It has a very ancient look & one would suppose that it might be sacred enough to be secure. I have long known that the Mich. 2d had no fear or reverence as a general thing for God or the places where he is worshipped but I hoped that the memory of Gen. Washington might protect almost anything with which it was associated. I believe our soldiers would have torn the church down in 2 days. They were all over it in less than 10 minutes tearing off the ornaments, splitting the wood work [off] the pews, knocking the bricks to pieces & everything else they could get at. They wanted pieces to carry away.

I do not believe there is a civilized nation on the earth which has so little appreciation of the beautiful & sacred as ours. In the madness of the French Revolution mobs not one in a hundred of whom could read or write, not a man of them was known to injure a work of art or violate a place sacred by association. A more absolute set of vandals than our men can not be found on the face of the earth. As true as I am living I believe they would steal Washington's coffin if they could get to it. What else can you expect of men who will steal even from an enemy family pictures, daguerreotypes, family bibles, records and such like articles.

"A more absolute set of vandals than our men can not be found on the face of the earth."

PRIVATE JACOB W. BARTMESS
39TH INDIANA MOUNTED INFANTRY

Bartmess enlisted in the fall of 1862, just ahead of the first Federal draft. He had little interest in military service, but he fought honorably at Murfreesboro, where he was captured, and after being exchanged he fought with Sherman in the campaign through Georgia. Concerned mainly with the health of his wife, Amanda, and their two children, he wrote home frequently.

Camp Drake.
Near Murfreesboro Ten.
Sunday—June 7th. 1863.
My kind affectionate Wife—.

Amanda let me assure you that this place bears the marks of battle. Where once stood the nice dwelling of the rich planter and the negro huts, and the good fencing which enclosed the large rich farm and separated it into fields. now is a vast ruin. there are no houses, no negro huts, no fencing. One vast desolation exists for many miles around. The trees are wonderfly marked with minie-balls. Some of them from the thickness of my body down are entirely cout down with canon balls. But what is more: the many little boards which stick in the ground in regular rotation, marking the spot where lies the boddies of of hundreds of our brave men. who fell a sacrifice on their countries, altar on stoneriver's bloody field. My thoughts ask me where are the many little orphans calling and crying for pappy, while his body is mouldering in this vast grave yard. And where is that widowed, and heartbroken wife, who when the question is forced on her mind where is my husband? and the answer comes that he fell and was burried by careless hands on stonerivers battle field. Writhes in desperate and indescribable anguish. O. who will answer for the sin of this most dreadful and calamitous war. but why should I continue thus. God bless the right.

J. W. Bartmess.

Receipts from the Confederacy (top) and Union (bottom) promise
restitution for the extensive damage done to Ferry Hill, the Wash-
ington County, Maryland, farm of the Reverend Robert Douglas.
But the Confederate receipt was worthless after the war, and the
Federal government demanded proof of loyalty before making good.
For Douglas—the father of Henry Kyd Douglas, a member of
Stonewall Jackson's staff—this was impossible.

LIEUTENANT ALEXANDER T. BARCLAY
4TH VIRGINIA INFANTRY

*In late December 1861 Stonewall Jackson launched a series of raids into Mary-
land and western Virginia to disrupt Union supply lines along the Chesapeake
& Ohio Canal. Nearly two months later, after a grueling 21-mile march over
snow-covered roads, Jackson's troops, including Barclay's regiment, made their
winter camp in the western Virginia town of Romney, recently sacked and
vacated by Union troops. "Of all the miserable holes in creation," Barclay wrote
upon seeing the remains, "Romney takes the lead."*

January the 25th, 1862
  Dear Sister, . . .
  After knocking about there a day or so, we came back to the Cross
Roads in charge of the prisoners. When at the Cross Roads we again
joined the regiment and marched to Bloomering, a small village in the
Romney road. We staid there all night.

The next morning we went to town and took our pick of the houses,
if indeed there was any choice, as all are too filthy for decent men to
stay in, and I stayed there some time, expecting every day to have to
move to the river to capture some Yankees who were reported to be at
Patterson's Creek on this side of the Potomac. But they had planked
the railroad bridge and managed to get away, which is a great pity, for if
ever men deserved to be hung it was this band of cut throats.

There are not less than fifty or sixty houses burnt around Romney
and cattle, hogs and horses shot down and left lying.

One man was shot whilst making shoes in his house and the house
was burnt over him, although his wife and children begged the dogs to
allow them to take his body out of the house before they burnt it; and a
poor old woman who lived near Romney had her home burnt down and
when she asked them to allow her to save some things they told her to
take out whatever she pleased. She took out some bedding and an old
clock. After the house was burnt they set fire to the things which she
had taken out and burnt them, too.

Hampshire County is just a wilderness now. You see only ashes
where a few weeks ago beautiful houses stood. . . .

Good bye, Ted

CAPTAIN GEORGE K. PARDEE

42D OHIO INFANTRY

Pardee was acutely sensitive to the human misery he encountered in the South—especially the suffering of children. Determined to build a better life for his wife, Caroline, and their son, Karl, whom he missed fiercely, he read for the law in his spare time. After being mustered out in 1864 he passed the bar, built a law practice, and had three more children with Caroline.

How terribly the inhabitants of the revolted states must suffer and yet we cannot have peace honorably until many more young men are slain or mangled to maintain the honor and dignity of the nation. Oh, what a deluded race of people we are and yet think ourselves enlightened and civilized. Shame on us.

Capt. Riggs and I called on a house last night near here. We found three little girls, the oldest one ten years, and a poor widow woman (her husband died in the rebel army) huddled around a cheerless fire, half frightened at our coming, two little girls about as old as our nieces with no shoes or anything in the clothing line but little ragged calico dresses. The other and the mother had very little better clothing. She said she had very little cornmeal and nothing else to eat, had some money. She got washing for the soldiers, I think very little, not enough to buy shoes for the children, she said. It has been very cold for two or three days, was very cold last night. I never suffered more in Ohio, and how such little children can live is a wonder to me. Most all the inhabitants are destitute here in town. It must be awful outside our lines. I feel very sorry for the helpless children, but I can do nothing to help them. I hope and pray that my little family shall never be left in such circumstances, may heaven forbid it. Oh, is this not a horrible war, Cal.

Just 19 years old when the war broke out, Caroline "Carrie" Pardee had more to worry about than just her husband, George. She had two brothers in the Union army; one served time as a prisoner of war.

"She got washing for the soldiers, I think very little, not enough to buy shoes for the children, she said."

PRIVATE JOHN A. POTTER
101st Illinois Infantry

The experience Potter relates in this excerpt from his memoirs occurred in December 1862, shortly after he was mustered into the army. Later that month he and much of his regiment were captured at Holly Springs, Mississippi, in a Rebel cavalry raid and spent six months as paroled prisoners of war in Missouri. After the war Potter became a Methodist minister.

In a photograph most likely taken near Manassas, Virginia, women wait to receive rations from Federal authorities. Many dispossessed Southerners had to rely on Union handouts, an experience made all the more distasteful by the Federal government's insistence that they first sign loyalty oaths.

At Grand Junction there was an alarm raised of rebels threatening the road, so we were detained for the night. The troops there were kept under arms all night, in case of an attack. A flat car had been barricaded and two cannon mounted on it. The artillerymen were old veterans and seemed to enjoy the prospect for a fight, so they could try their guns from their fort on wheels, as they called it. It was a bitter cold night. My chum and I were compelled to leave our bed in the ambulance and go to a large, blazing fire near by, that the battery boys kept feeding with good, fine lumber, as there were thousands of feet stacked up in a lumber yard close by. I enjoyed the warmth of the fire, but my nature revolted at the wasteful destruction of such valuable lumber. The battery boys were very kind to us. Our rations were rather scant, and they gave us a supply of hard bread, of which they seemed to have no lack. We boiled a kettle of coffee, and were told to make ourselves welcome to their fire and not freeze to death on the cars. We were pleased to share their kind hospitality; but some colored men who had come in to escape the toils of bondage did not fare so well. I never could understand the antipathy of some white men towards the colored race; their detestation of them, on account of color, and their delight in torturing them. Our hosts were men of this type. They were lavish in their kindness to us, but cruel to the unfortunate men of color. These poor runaways begged to stop and warm at the roaring fire. They were told rudely they might warm awhile, and soon depart, for they did not want them there. The poor men sank down by the fire, and, seeming in a very exhausted state, were soon snoring, fast asleep. Soon one of the battery men, annoyed by the loud snoring, said: "Look at them niggers, gone fast asleep! They said they'd go directly, and they've taken up quarters for the night. Come, boys, let's cook them!" and, to my great horror, proceeded to drag the negroes through the blazing fire. I could hardly reconcile their cruelty to them to the great kindness they had shown us. Can the casuist explain how such a streak of the milk of human kindness and such a display of ferocious cruelty unite in one breast? Thus I was touched on two sides of my nature, but was powerless to obviate the cruelty shown the colored men because we had been the recipients of great favors at the hands of the offenders, and all parties were entire strangers to us. Truly the phenomena of human nature is the greatest mystery of the universe.

LIEUTENANT DAVID E. JOHNSTON
7TH VIRGINIA INFANTRY

At a time when the war was going badly for the Confederacy, the 1864 Christmas dinner provided by the ladies of Virginia gave a much-needed morale boost. In his memoirs, written nearly 50 years after the war, Johnston warmly remembered the contributions made by Southern women. "For them," he wrote, "no sacrifice was too great."

Christmas, 1864, was approaching and extensive preparations were being made by city, town and country to furnish the army of Northern Virginia a Christmas dinner, the women taking the lead—God bless them! The newspapers urged the movement forward, commit-

tees were appointed to collect and forward the good things to the soldiers. The papers proclaimed that Virginia, devastated as she was by an invading host, was yet able to feed her soldiers; that the cattle upon a thousand hills were hers. Though the cattle were not there, the day came, and with it a bountiful supply which made us glad, and we thanked our benefactors and took courage.

The credit for our Christmas dinner was due the women. In every movement for the uplift and betterment of our race, and in every worthy cause, woman is the first to espouse, the last to forsake. Having once fixed her affections upon the object of our cause, her love therefor became as fast and enduring as the rock-ribbed hills.

PRIVATE ISAAC HERMANN
MARTIN'S BATTERY, GEORGIA LIGHT ARTILLERY

Though difficult to adjust to at first, the army way of life—including sleeping on the ground—quickly became second nature to soldiers. And as Private Hermann related in his memoirs, the military habits were hard to break. Born in France, Hermann came to America shortly before the war and settled in Washington County, in central Georgia. Once the fighting began, he quickly volunteered to defend his adopted home.

When alighting from the train and seeing all those good things prepared for us, I at once took my position. A lady remarked, "Help yourself." I took hold of a piece of fowl, and as I was about to take a bite, someone struck me on the arm with such force that the piece of fowl dropped out of my hand, and someone said, "Those things are not for you." It was Mayor Wilkins. He was glad to see me, and said, "I have something better for you, boys. How many of the First Georgia are here? Get them all together and follow me." We were about a dozen of the old Washington Rifles. He conducted us to a room where we met a committee of gentlemen. After the usual shaking hands and introductions, we passed into another chamber. I never beheld a more bountiful and artistically prepared spread. Provisions arranged on a revolving table, shelved to a pyramid, and loaded with delicious wines. In a corner of the room was a table covered with case liquors of every description, and some fine cigars. I was astonished, I had no idea such delicacies could have been gotten in the whole Confederacy. We surely did enjoy the hospitality of the Committee. Mayor Wilkins introduced me to a Mr.

> "The two years service I had seen, made a feather bed rather an impediment to my repose, having become accustomed to sleep out doors on the hard ground, with my knapsack as a pillow."

Rothschild, saying, "I want you to take good care of him, he is a splendid fellow." Turning to me he said, "Hermann, I want you to stay all night with this gentleman, he will treat you all right.". . . I was royally treated; the lady of the house and daughter played on the piano and sang. I joined in the chorus 'till late in the night, when I was shown to my room, nicely furnished, a nice clean feather bed and all the requisites for comfort, but I could not sleep, I did not lay comfortable. The two years service I had seen, made a feather bed rather an impediment to my repose, having become accustomed to sleep out doors on the hard ground, with my knapsack as a pillow, so I got up, put my knap sack under my head and lay by the side of the bed on the carpet, and slept like a log the balance of the night; so soundly, that I did not hear the negro boy who was sent to my room to blacken my boots, open the door, but I heard a noise like someone slamming the door and I heard someone running down stairs. I heard many voices talking, and someone coming up stairs, opening the door very unceremoniously, I looked—there was Mr. Rothschild,—greatly astonished and laughing, he could hardly talk. Finally he said, "What in the world made you lay on the floor." I explained to him that being no longer used to sleeping on a bed, I could not rest until I got on the hard floor. Then he told me he had sent up a boy to blacken my boots, who had scared them all by telling them that the man up stairs had fallen off of the bed and lay dead on the floor. I took my ablution, and went down to breakfast, all enjoying that I was still able to do justice to the meal that my kind host and hostess set before me.

Confederate soldiers quickly learned that they could augment their meager rations with donations from sympathetic civilians. In this drawing by Lieutenant William L. Sheppard of the Richmond Howitzers, a pair of Rebels beg a local woman for some buttermilk.

EDWARD C. TURNER
FARMER, FAUQUIER COUNTY, VIRGINIA

Though his brother, Thomas, was an officer in the Federal navy, Edward Turner makes clear his low opinion of Union soldiers in this journal entry from 1862. A prominent Fauquier County farmer, Turner had the misfortune to live in an area of Virginia that frequently shifted between Union and Confederate control. The troops mentioned in this entry—including Turner's two sons—are under the command of Stonewall Jackson and are on their way to Second Manassas.

Tuesday, August 26.
. . . At an early hour the head of the column comes in view advancing rapidly from toward Salem. All day long our house and yard are filled with soldiers hungry, thirsty, barefooted and some of

"How many now passing with light and careless hearts will 'ere another week be citizens of the unknown world?"

PRIVATE ROBERT A. JARMAN
27TH MISSISSIPPI INFANTRY

A three-year veteran of the Army of Tennessee, Jarman was one of only four men left in his company by the end of the Battle of Nashville in December 1864. The army briefly wintered in Tupelo, Mississippi, then left for Montgomery, Alabama, in February of 1865, where Jarman's company was mustered out. According to his account, even mustering out was an ordeal.

them almost naked, but bright and buoyant asking only a mouthful to eat and to be lead against the enemy. The people everywhere relieve them to the utmost of their ability but having been severely plundered by the Feds., little and in many instances nothing is left to feast them on, they take gratefully however, whatever is given and go on rejoicing in the prospect of speedily driving the enemy from their soil and the return of sweet peace. Among those who arrive for a scanty meal are our two sons Tom and Beverley, our nephew Wilson and several of our Randolph cousins. We thank God from the bottom of our hearts for the return of our dear boys and for His kind protection of them during their absence. They remain but a few moments and move on. In a day or two they are to meet the enemy in deadly conflict. How many now passing with light and careless hearts will 'ere another week be citizens of the unknown world? May God have mercy upon their noble souls. Our own dear boys may never return to their once peaceful and happy home. With fervent prayer we commend them to God who alone has power to protect and save them. How marked is the difference between the Federal and Confederate soldiers. The latter bland and courteous, asking in the most respectful manner for the gratification of his simple wants and returning heart felt thanks for the trifle he receives. The former rough and rude, frequently domineering and insulting, demanding instead of asking to be fed and insolent and huffish after he is filled. The difference is easily explained. The Confederate in nine instances out of ten is the very cream and flower of our population. He is well-bred and cultivated. The Federal, if not a low foreigner is from the meaner class of the Yankee nation, than whom the world contains no people more selfish, unprincipled and degraded. The one is brave and patriotic; the other is cowardly and mercenary, the one is fighting for a principle dearer than life itself; the other for the miserable stipend allowed for his services. 'Tis not remarkable under these circumstances that victory in so large a majority of engagements perched upon the Confederate banner, even when the disparity of forces is equal to two or three and sometimes five or ten to one.

We moved to Montgomery, Alabama, where we were encamped out beyond the State House, and were told not to cut any timber in the woods where we were, as it belonged to a crippled Confederate soldier, and that there would be wood hauled us. At first wood was hauled us, but we soon found out that the land did not belong to a crippled soldier, but to a man that had on his gin breast, in large brass letters, "Hon. Bolen Hall," but we did not think him honorable, for while we were there, there was a long rainy spell, and it rained very hard, and he would not even let the men at night sleep under his gin house, or in it, and the two brigades, when they found out, and all about him, eat up his market garden. While here at Montgomery, we were mustered, and had to make out our muster rolls. Then Lieutenant Welch of Company L, 27th Mississippi, and myself put on our nicest clothes, blacked our shoes, and went to Mr. Hall's house and asked for the use of a table in his back hall to write on, when we were told that his daughters were at home that day, and to come next week and he would accomodate us. When told the urgency of the case, he said his daughters were at home, and shut the door in our face, and then we were forced to go more than a mile, through a hard rain, to Montgomery, to do our writing. And when, after the surrender, we came home and saw that the Federal cavalry had been there and burned his gin house and cotton bales for him, no one felt sorry.

SURGEON SPENCER G. WELCH
13TH SOUTH CAROLINA INFANTRY

The summer of 1863 found Welch confident for the future of the Confederacy. His spirits were further buoyed by the sumptuous dinner he chanced upon while camped in Virginia. The next day his regiment left for Gettysburg. Welch survived the battle and served through the war, surrendering with his regiment at Appomattox.

Cordelia Strother Welch of Fruit Hill, a plantation in Saluda County, South Carolina, turned 22 the day South Carolina troops fired on Fort Sumter, April 12, 1861. She had been married barely a year before her husband joined the army in 1862; while he was away their two-year-old son, George, died.

A while after we stopped I started off to one of these farmhouses for the purpose of getting my dinner, as I was quite hungry, and wanted something different from what I had been accustomed to most of the time on the march. On going to the house a very nice, smiling young girl met me at the door, and, upon my making known my wishes, she very pleasantly said she "guessed" so; but said they already had agreed to accommodate a good many, and that they would do the best they could by us all if I would return at four o'clock.

This I did, and found Adjutant Reedy of the Fourteenth Regiment and several others of my acquaintance. Reedy, being quite a young man, talked a good deal to the girl. I was hungry as a wolf, but when I came to the table and viewed what was upon it my hunger was aggravated more than ever. It seemed that there was no end to everything that was good. We had nice fried ham, stewed chicken, excellent biscuit, lightbread, butter, buckwheat cakes that were most delicious, molasses, four or five different kinds of preserves and several other dishes. We also had plenty of good coffee and cold, rich milk to drink. None but a soldier who has experienced a hard campaign can conceive of how a gang of hungry men could appreciate such a meal. I must say that this late dinner was a perfect Godsend.

After we had finished eating I felt ashamed to offer them Confederate money, but could do no better, and offered it with an apology. They very readily accepted it, and when I insisted that they should take a dollar they refused and would have only fifty cents. This house was guarded to prevent our men committing depredations such as they had been doing, and which was having a demoralizing effect upon the army. Soldiers must be made to behave or they will not fight.

SERGEANT JAMES P. SULLIVAN

6TH WISCONSIN INFANTRY

"Mickey" Sullivan was wounded four times and was the only man in his regiment to reenlist twice. But his comrades valued him as much for his wit as his tenacity; his captain once remarked that "for genuine sallies of humor at unexpected times, I never saw his equal." Writing for a Wisconsin newspaper in 1884, Sullivan recounted an 1863 scouting mission. The "B" of the story is Lieutenant Edward Brooks.

In May, 1863, the 8th Illinois cavalry was sent on a scout down that strip of Virginia lying between the Potomac and the Rappahannock rivers, called by the natives the "Northern Neck," and the 2d regiment went along to cover their rear and assist them to collect hams, chickens, corn dodgers, mutton, fresh pork and anything else eatable. . . .

Lincoln's famous proclamation had been issued the New Years before and the kid glove policy had been abandoned to a considerable extent, and wherever our flag went it brought liberty and emancipation to the colored people, and, though the slaveocracy did their best to prevent the dissemination of the news, by some underground process the slaves had become pretty generally informed that "Massa Linkum"

would receive all who came. The district in which we were had hitherto almost escaped the "iron hoofs" of war, and was in a comparatively flourishing condition, and being well stocked with slaves, the negroes flocked to us in droves. Such a medley of sights and sounds as our brigade presented on that march was probably seldom witnessed during the war. Ox carts with one ox and a cow for the motive power, family carriages, mules, donkeys, darkies of all ages, sizes and complexions, "toting" on their heads feather beds, bed clothes, stoves, wash tubs, iron kettles, household goods of all kinds, clothing, crockery and anything else their fancy and avarice prompted; and cavalry "mud waders," darkies, donk[ies] and all were indiscriminately strung along the line of march for miles. Soldiers carrying hams on their bayonets (that the dripping might fall on the rank behind,) chickens, turkeys, ducks, geese, alive and dead, hind quarters of sheep and hogs, eggs, butter, milk, corn dodgers, and raw corn meal. . . .

The "staff" of our regiment had a peculiar weakness for piazzas, and when the shadows of evening began to lengthen their eagle eyes (when not dimmed with tears at the recollection of that pitcher of cider which their host of last night did not produce,) would eagerly scan the route of march for piazzas. When one apparently suitable was discovered, B would gallantly ride forward to reconnoiter and on his return report as to the number and appearance of the young ladies, the prospects for coffee and corn bread (provided he furnished the coffee,) and sometimes, if he thought about it, would mention the suitability of the camp ground and the chances for wood and water. On the occasion referred to, the report was favorable and soon we went into bivouac. The staff started for the piazza and were met at the front steps by a daughter of the South of middle age and vinegary visage who welcomed them warmly; informed them that she was a widow; professed the strongest union sentiments; opened her parlor and piano; and ordered a boun-

"To fill the cup of their happiness, three young ladies of most exquisitely lovely forms and beautiful, smiling faces made their appearance."

teous supper to be prepared, while, to fill the cup of their happiness, three young ladies of most exquisitely lovely forms and beautiful, smiling faces made their appearance, and were presented to the staff by their doting mamma. Evadne, the eldest of the trio, who was musically inclined, seated herself at the piano and began soothing the days of war with the "Star Spangled banner" and kindred melodies. Louise, the next in rank, who had made a specialty of history, regaled them with a correct recital of the life and times of Washington, while the flaxen haired youngest daughter, attracted by B's resemblance to herself in capillary adornments, approached and engaged him in a most bewitching conversation. The gallant hero, who had stood undaunted in a dozen battle fields, was hopelessly overpowered by the "magic of beauty" and surrendered at discretion, and made no effort to conceal his admiration, which was apparently reciprocated. It was evidently a case of love at first sight. I dare not say what visions of plantations, and cotton bales, tobacco and sugar cane with Evangeline gracefully swinging in a hammock, "when this cruel war was over," flitted through his mind as he listened to the music of her soft voice.

But outside, the officers who trailed the puissant "toad sticker" on foot and we of the musket and knapsack made our fires, boiled our coffee, fried our "bung slide" and commented on the singularity of the fact that at this plantation there were no contrabands to greet us with grins and glittering ivories and shining eyes glistening like new constellations in the southern sky. Except a few house servants who manifested no signs of welcome, there were no negroes about the place. At length Jones of Co. E, who was prowling around in search of poultry, spied, away up in the garret, dark faces and wooly polls protruding through a window. The news spread, a ladder was raised and down came a troop of Africans, some thirty-five or forty in number, whom their mistress vainly believed were safely hidden from the prying eyes of the hated Yan-

kees. But soon she heard of the discovery and, oh, my countrymen, what a change was there. Her black eyes flashed fire, her vinegary face grew more acid (gone were her welcoming smiles,) and with a voice as sweet as an army fife concert, she eloquently and forcible ordered the staff in true southern phrase to git "Out of this house, you Northern mudsills, you infernal Yankee Nigger thieves; you robbers; you desecrators of our southern soil; you cowardly hirelings." and word was immediately sent to the kitchen for Dinah to stop the "chicken doins." Evadne's turn up nose elevated itself still higher. Bang went the lid on her piano and in a tone yet shriller than her mother's, she, too, ordered the staff to git, and the historian, in a very energetic style of elocution, informed them of every defeat the union army had sustained and confidently predicted for them a dog's death at the hands of her chivalric southern army. But, "oh, frailty, thy name is woman;" it was whispered among us outsiders that Evangeline seized "B" by the hair with the fair hands he had been admiring, and there is no saying what the result would have been had not some one interposed and released poor "B."

Sullenly the staff left the room; slowly they retired to the far end of the piazza; sadly they ordered their servants to prepare supper of coffee, bacon and hardtack. But no power could drive them from that piazza; that was their last ditch, and there they resolved to stay or die. Also, for visions of Evangeline in the hammock and Northern Neck Plantations, gone like the baseless fabric of a dream! To us who had been the innocent cause of that tempest and who heard with affright the shrill voices of the ladies and beheld with awe the staff retreat, the newly emancipated brought hoe-cake and eatables innumerable and unlike the staff we had reason to rejoice in our "chicken doins."

For days "B's" usually genial countenance wore a look of settled gloom that not even a rumored extra issue of commissary could wholly remove.

ASSISTANT SURGEON RICHARD L. JOHNSON
15TH SOUTH CAROLINA INFANTRY

Fancying himself quite a ladies' man, Johnson teased a girlfriend back home with the following letter. There is no record of her reply. A week later, in anticipation of his return home, he wrote his grandmother and asked her to hint to the local ladies that "an old aunt of mine out here has given me a hundred thousand dollars."

Near Raccoon Ford Va.
June 5th 1863
My Dear little Sweet-heart,
. . . I am going to tell you what I did yesterday. I know it will amuse, and show you that I deserve my reputation, both here and at home, of being a great lover of that fickle, deceitful, bewitching race of creatures who wear petticoats and lead poor men astray. Well after walking 18 miles yesterday, and about the time that my knapsack had, in my imagination, grown from 20 to 120 lbs. in weight, about the time that I began to feel hot, tired, foot-sore, and weary, I came to a mill, where the water was pouring over in a style that tempted me to perform certain ablutions. While enjoying myself immensely with my breeches rolled up, I noticed on the bank quite a bevy of young ladies. I did not care much and concluded I could stand it if they could. After I had had out my fun in that line, I put my shoes on and went up and joined the ladies. There were seven in all—two married and the rest young lassies, from fifteen to twenty eight. I only fell in love with two of them. One a sweet little soul with blue eyes &c &c. The other an even finer looking girl, and very intelligent. As their home was only 2 1/2 from the road, and I had walked only 18 miles that day, I concluded to see the little ducks to their domicile; which charatable errand I performed to my entire satisfaction, and, to judge by the sweet and coquettish smile the little blue eyed sinner threw back over her shoulder through her bright locks, I suppose it was to her satisfaction too. I took tea with them, and never left till 9 o'clock. Fortune favored me however, for the regiment had gone only five miles farther, and I got into a wagon which took me two miles on my way. Now that is being a gallant youth—is it not?

The presence of women in an army camp kindled great excitement and curiosity on the part of the soldiers, as depicted in this postwar drawing by William Sheppard.

"Many a rough, rugged nature felt softened and uplifted after meeting these purehearted girls."

SERGEANT MAJOR WILLIAM P. CHAMBERS
46TH MISSISSIPPI INFANTRY

Despite the limited educational opportunities available in rural Mississippi, William Chambers read widely and became a schoolteacher in 1859. He fought at Vicksburg and was wounded at the Battle of Allatoona, Georgia, in 1864. Owing to his injury, he remained behind as his unit and the rest of the Army of Tennessee were virtually destroyed at Franklin and Nashville.

In the afternoon of Saturday last, the students of the Female Seminary at Summerfield (some six miles distant) came in a body to "see the soldiers." It was a charming sight to see so many lovely girls just budding into a lovelier womanhood all dressed in uniform, their hands filled with flowers, their faces wreathed in smiles, their eyes sparkling with girlish gaiety, and yet with sweet, womanly sympathy turned upon the weather-beaten Mississippi boys, while their lips gave utterances to many of a hopeful, helpful word. Many a rough, rugged nature felt softened and uplifted after meeting these purehearted girls. Not being over gallant by nature, and less so by practice, I failed to receive any of the bouquets that were so lavishly dispensed, often accompanied by dainty little scraps of paper on which a tender thought or fervent wish was traced.

LIEUTENANT COLONEL THEODORE LYMAN
STAFF, MAJOR GENERAL GEORGE G. MEADE

While encamped for the winter near Brandy Station, Lieutenant Colonel Lyman was summoned by Major General Andrew A. Humphreys, Meade's chief of staff, to squire a group of officers' wives on a round of visits to several corps and division headquarters. He was joined by Captain Adolfo Cavada of Humphreys' staff and later recorded his misadventures in his journal.

Headquarters Army of Potomac
January 29, 1864
If you saw the style of officers' wives that come here, I am sure you would wish to stay away. *Quelle expérience* had I yesterday! I was nearly bored to death, and was two hours and a half late for my dinner. Oh, list to my harrowing tale. I was in my tent, with my coat off, neatly mending my maps with a little paste, when Captain Cavada poked in his head (he was gorgeous in a new frock-coat). "Colonel," said he, "General Humphreys desires that you will come and help entertain some ladies!" I held up my pasty hands in horror, and said, "What!" "Ladies!" quoth Cavada with a grin; "a surprise party on horseback, thirteen ladies and about thirty officers." There was no *moyen;* I washed my hands, put on the double-breaster, added a cravat, and proceeded, with a sweet smile, to the tent, whence came a sound of revelry and champagne corks. Such a set of feminine humans I have not seen often; it was Lowell factories broken loose and gone mad. They were all gotten up in some sort of long thing, to ride in. One had got a lot of orange tape and trimmed her jacket in the dragoon style; another had the badge of the Third Corps pinned all askew in her hat; a third had a major's knot worked in tarnished lace on her sleeve; while a fourth had garnitured her chest by a cape of grey squirrel-skin. And there was General Humphreys, very red in the face, smiling like a basket of chips, and hopping round with a champagne bottle, with all the spring of a boy of sixteen. He spied me at once, and introduced me to a Mrs. M——, who once married somebody who treated her very badly and afterwards fortunately went up; so Mrs. M—— seemed determined to make up lost time and be jolly in her liberty. She was quite bright; also quite warm and red in the face, with hard riding and, probably, champagne. Then they said they would go over to General Sedgwick's, and General Humphreys asked if I would not go, too, which invitation it was not the thing to refuse; so I climbed on my horse, with the malicious consolation that it would be fun to see poor, modest Uncle John with such a load! But Uncle John, though blushing and overcome, evidently did not choose to be put upon; so, with great politeness, he offered them sherry, with naught to eat and no champagne. Then nothing would do but go to Headquarters of the 3d Corps, whither, to my horror, the gallant Humphreys would gang likewise. Talk about cavalry raids to break down horses! If you want to do that, put a parcel of women on them and set them going across the country. Such a Lützow's wild hunt hath not been seen since the day of the respected L. himself! Finally one lady's horse ran away, and off went the brick,

Humphreys, like a shot, to stop her. Seeing her going into a pine tree, he drove his horse between the tree and her; but, in so doing, encountered a hidden branch, which slapped the brisk old gent out of his saddle, like a shuttle-cock! The Chief-of-Staff was up in a second, laughing at his mishap; while I galloped up, in serious alarm at his accident. To make short a long story, the persistent H. tagged after those womenfolk (and I tagged after *him*) first to Corps Headquarters, then to General Carr's Headquarters, and finally to General Morris's Headquarters, by which time it was dark! I was the only one that knew the nearest way home (we were four miles away) and didn't I lead the eminent soldier through runs and mud-holes, the which he do hate!

LIEUTENANT ABNER R. SMALL
16TH MAINE INFANTRY

After retreating from Fredericksburg, Small's regiment set up camp at Falmouth, Virginia, in January 1863. Although in this account he and his bunkmate are annoyed at being put out for a night by some female travelers, their discomfort was nothing compared to what awaited them. By the 20th the regiment had broken camp to take part in the Mud March, in which Union troops tried to flank the enemy at Fredericksburg but were bogged down for four days in a vast quagmire.

The ground for our winter home was a gorge with a brook of good water running down the middle. Quite a grove of trees had to be felled, which were all utilized for houses and firewood. The men built log pens with a hearth at one end, and made flues of small sticks plastered with mud; then they fastened their tents over the pens, and set their fires going, and so had rooms that were high enough to stand in and fairly warm. Headquarters was established on a side hill, into which we dug for the foundation. At the back we made a neat fireplace; above it we built a chimney surmounted by a pork and lard barrel; and I remember that the barrel, when dry, often took fire and illuminated the entire camp.

Max and I built generously, and inside our finished house, in the warmth of a roaring blaze, we set up bedsteads, and overlaid them with pine boughs for mattresses, and covered the boughs with blankets for counterpanes. How proudly and fondly we gazed upon those beds! We had slept on the ground, between knolls, to keep from rolling down hill, in all kinds of weather, and now we were to have a heavenly rest secure above the sacred soil. We longed for night and measured with impatience the going down of the sun. Even the silvery voice of black Ben, announc-

Officers of Independent Battery H, Pennsylvania Light Artillery, entertain female visitors at their camp near Alexandria, Virginia. Organized in 1862, Battery H spent the war guarding Washington, D.C.

ing that tea was ready, failed to move us from rapt contemplation of those beds. Just as the sun began hiding itself, there came darkly into view a horse, then an ambulance, and in the ambulance two women, visitors.

"Oh, Lord of Hosts!" I groaned.

"Oh, Hell!" said Max.

We slept on the ground, or tried to; we lay in the cold frosts, beneath the stars, shivering under one poor blanket, and near enough to our ravished house to hear the visitors exclaim:

"What splendid beds these soldiers have!"

"How romantic it must be to sleep on boughs!"

Those women robbed us of our rest; they ate, for supper and breakfast, supplies that had cost us five dollars, and some things from home that we could not replace; and they left us nothing, hardly an acknowledgment of our courtesy. They rather conveyed an impression that it was they who had favored us. What they had come for, God only knows. Max said, later, that they did leave a cheap Testament and a calico blouse, and that Ben embellished the blouse with red tape and wore it as an undress uniform until the starch was out, when he used it for a dishcloth.

LUCY REBECCA BUCK

FRONT ROYAL, VIRGINIA

In May 1862 Brigadier General Nathan Kimball of the Federal army set up headquarters at Bel Air, the Buck family estate in Front Royal. Nineteen-year-old Lucy Buck, whose brother Irving served on the staff of Confederate general Patrick R. Cleburne, meticulously recorded every offense committed by the Yankee intruders.

While talking in Ma's room the band, a very fine brass one, had come up on the pavement and struck up an inspiring air, attracting a number of outsiders to the yard. The music was very fine and had the performers been any other than they were, I should have enjoyed it unspeakably. As it was, I liked it until they struck up "Yankee Doodle" and "Dixie"—that would not do any way as Nellie, Laura and I gave them to understand by turning our backs to the window

and dropping the curtains. They were requested to play the "Mocking Bird" in memory of Irvie and some other popular airs. They did not know them, but offered to go down to camp, practice the pieces and come back and perform them. They just played their old "Yankee Doodle" with so much gusto because they knew how obnoxious it had become to good Southerners. And as for "Dixie" 'tis the height of impudence in them to appropriate one of our national airs. We were a good deal provoked and I had just gone into Grandma's room to try and regain my temper by reading when another band more magnificent than the first commenced discoursing sweet music under the windows. Dear absent brothers!—when they played the "Mocking Bird," "Annie Laurie," "The Dearest Spot on Earth" and "Be Kind to the Loved Ones at Home"—songs so often sung together in our home in so many happier hours—I could not restrain my tears. Just then that hound old crocodile Freeman stepped forward on the porch and called out in an insulting tone—"Boys! boys!—you're no true Yankee soldiers if you could think of omitting to play 'Yankee Doodle.'" Whereupon they commenced vigorously playing the odious Yankee air a second time. Down went the curtains and down they remained until the musicians departed.

During the siege of Petersburg, Virginia, in 1864, Union general Gouverneur K. Warren's V Corps used the farmhouse of J. E. Avery as their headquarters. This drawing shows the officers of the V Corps dining by moonlight on the lawn of the Avery home.

"And what is worse, yes even than death itself, the Mothers, Wives & daughters of these men have become strangers to virtue and female modesty."

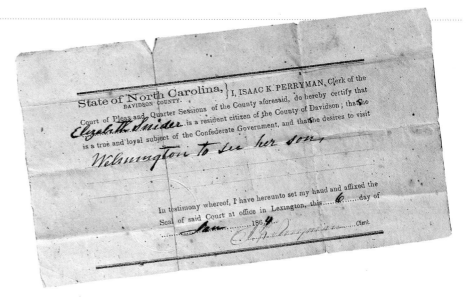

CAPTAIN DANIEL O'LEARY
15TH KENTUCKY (U.S.) INFANTRY

By the end of 1863 the number of Rebel deserters and the decimated state of the Army of Tennessee led Captain O'Leary to conclude that the Civil War would soon be over. Only peace, he felt, would improve living conditions for the people of the war-ravaged South. This letter to his wife must have generated mixed emotions, for her family was pro-South, and her brother served in the 2d Kentucky (C.S.) Mounted Infantry.

Chattanooga, Tenn.
December 29th 1863. . . .
Small squads of Rebs are brought in every few days. Mostly deserters who have got tired of fighting for their rights and wisely concluded to abandon the cause—which ambitious men thought them to be a just one—and seek peaceful homes north of the Ohio. In my humble judgement if the statements of these men are true the rebellion is about "played out." The sooner peace is restored the better for the southern people as they are the sufferers, driven from their homes, their property destroyed or taken for the use of the army. And what is worse, yes even than death itself, the Mothers, Wives & daughters of these men have become strangers to virtue and female modesty— which is the greatest ornament of the sex—worse than the most degraded creatures which abound in the cities of the north. I do not Know what the standard of morality was in this country before the rebellion but if it has been the means of bringing about the present state of depravity and vice its authors deserve the execrations of all honest people.

Both sides drastically curtailed the movements of civilians near the front, often making them virtual prisoners in their own homes. Any travel—especially across the lines—required a permit, like the one above, issued to Elizabeth Snider of central North Carolina in 1864 so she could visit her son in the Federal-occupied town of Washington, on the Carolina coast.

QUARTERMASTER SERGEANT ROBERT PATRICK
4TH MISSISSIPPI INFANTRY

The deputy sheriff of Port Hudson, Louisiana, Patrick originally resisted administrative duty because he felt his place was at the front. But after tasting battle at Shiloh he decided that "if I could honorably keep out of it that I would never go into another." While stationed briefly near Aberdeen, Mississippi, he began flirtations with local girls Fay Stuart and, much more seriously, Maggie Ross. Though he wrote of the possibility of seeing Maggie again someday, there is no record he ever did so before his death in 1866.

I have had a good time since I have been at this camp. I have had a good comfortable bed to sleep in every cold night that has come and I have had a pleasant time with the girls in the neighborhood. I have carried on a heavy flirtation with Maggie and she and I are as loving as any two beings can be. I believe she loves me though it is hard to tell. One thing is that she allows me take a great many liberties with her which I do not think she would allow anyone else to take.

Sunday, December 25: This is destined to be a dull Christmas to all hands in camp though I have passed the time pleasantly enough with the girls.

Monday, December 26: It is rumored that we are to leave this place before a great while. I will be loath to go because I have the best kind of quarters and besides that, Maggie and I are getting along very well indeed the particulars of which I shall give at some future time.

I have sent out several times for some whiskey but have failed to get it, and I presume that it will be better if I don't get it. The day is dreadfully cold and gloomy.

I am teaching Maggie Phonography so that she can correspond with me in that style when I go away.

I have bid farewell to Miss Stuart in the way of a flirtation, because I have already as much as I can attend to with Maggie and it is impossible to carry on both at once. Maggie is very affectionate and I have a good deal of pleasure in her society.

Tuesday, December 27: We were ordered to Columbus, Mississippi this morning, and about 2 p. m. we left camp. I went up to Mr. Ross's and bid the family farewell, and Maggie let me hug her and kiss her for perhaps the last time. Maggie says that she never will forget me and I do not believe that she will for I never talked to any woman in my life as I did to her. She says that she never had any man to presume to say such things to her as I did, and that what astonished her so much was that she should take it up and carry it on with me. I told her that the reason was because she loved me and had the same confidence in me that she would have if I were her husband. I know that if she did not love me that she would not have let things go on as they did.

One night I had a great notion to seduce her, but I didn't do it. There is one thing that I have resolved never to do, and that is to seduce a girl and if I should allow my passions to get the better of my judgment, I will marry the girl that I slept with. I could have seduced Maggie for I had gained her entire confidence and she had come to think that everything I said and did was all right and looked up to me in everything. It was with a heavy heart that I left her, for I had formed quite an attachment for her and I was sorry to leave her and she was sorry to see me go. Perhaps I may meet her again before the war is over. She is a smart, active intelligent girl, and will make some man an excellent wife, but I could not think of marrying her. She gave me a lock of her hair before we parted.

Private Alfred Bellard drew this sketch of a woman on a swing "displaying a goodly proportion of leg" while he was on an 1863 outing near Washington, D.C. By this time Bellard was a member of the Veteran Reserve Corps, serving out the last months of his enlistment.

Ten generals attended the March 1863 wedding of Nellie Hammond and Captain Daniel Hart of the 7th New Jersey Volunteers, depicted at left. When Hart was denied leave, his fiancée gamely traveled to Fredericksburg to be married barely a mile from the front. Despite the conditions, the regiment took great pains to decorate the camp—including an altar fashioned from drums—and threw a festive dinner after the ceremony.

SURGEON DAVID G. GODWIN
WRIGHT'S BRIGADE, ARMY OF TENNESSEE

In between fighting and marching, soldiers often found time for romance. The soft spot Godwin displays for marriage may reflect the fact that he had proposed to his sweetheart on the day he enlisted but had to wait until the end of the war to marry her. During the war he cared for the wounded at Missionary Ridge and at Franklin, where he worked for three straight days without sleep.

*I*n The field
Atlanta, Ga. August 25th 1864
Miss Bettie, You will probably be somewhat astonished when I tell you that a great many Georgia ladies are marrying. I was at a wedding a few nights since—Rev Mr Page officiated. The Bridegroom was an enlisted man about twenty five years of age and a member of Capt Carnes old Battery—the Bride was a widow of about thirty five or forty Summers & resides in the city. Also a young lady came out on the lines where the Minnie balls were falling in profusion—and was there married to her soldier lover only some five days ago. This I considered rather a dangerous, romantic affair—don't you think so? Thus you see that love masters all fears & braves *any kind* of danger.

When have you heard from John or Jo? I know that John will be properly cared for at his mother's. I hope your own health has been restored. We are looking for Mr D Every day. Trust I will hear from you by him. I hope you are still well.

As Ever D——

LIEUTENANT EDWIN WELLER
107TH NEW YORK INFANTRY

For the duration of his service—nearly three years—Edwin Weller courted Antoinette Watkins back home in Havana, New York. This 1864 letter to "Nettie" is both teasing and earnest; although he jokes of the prospects of landing a "Southern Bell," he reassures her that his heart belongs to her. They were married after he returned home.

To Nettie Watkins
From Camp of Detachment 107 N.Y.V.
Near *Wartrace, Tenn.*
Feby 10th, 1864

Dear Friend Nett, . . .

I saw two very fine looking young ladies there who were in a store trading. Of course I wanted to get a peep at the gay damsels, so stepped in the store pretending I wanted to buy something and inquired for an article that I knew they did not have. I got a good glimpse of them and found out before I left who they were and where they lived.

You are pretty near right in thinking that we soldiers like the ladies as well as they do us. If we did not we would be singular beings I think. If the ladies think as much of us as we do of them they think considerable of us.

So for there being more "hearts than lives lost" here, during our stay in the South, I can not say. I have no doubt but there will be some hearts lost but I imagin the loss will be mostly among the ladies, for the soldiers as a general thing do not think them quite equal to the "Girls they left behind them," and all I have got to say to them is, if any of them are foolish enough to fall in love with me, they must pick themselves up again.

I fear if we all should follow the example of that soldier of the 46th and return with each a Southern Bell on his arm, there would be many wounded hearts among the northern ladies. And of course we do not wish to cause any more misery than there is now among the fair sex. And then it would be injuring the cause too much in the north—you perceive, don't you? that I am looking to you northern ladies interest, it is so. . . .

I have just had to stop writing to entertain a couple of ladies who came here to get a pass. They were very sociable. One was a married lady and the other was a young lady and a relative of the married lady. I was joking with them about hardtack. I told her it was a bargan and I would give her all the hardtack she wanted in exchange. The young lady said she liked my quarters pretty well but thought she would not stay. So I did not make such a bargan after all.

Antoinette "Nettie" Watkins as she appeared in 1864.

"There were many men in the army who would rather pay twenty five cents for a letter than to write it themselves."

Letter carriers pose with their mail wagon at Brandy Station in 1864. The previous year Union general Joseph Hooker instituted bureaucratic reforms that greatly increased the reliability of the mail, which was vital to a soldier's morale.

PRIVATE A. MORRIS
2D OHIO INFANTRY

This account of how the mail was delivered during the war appeared in an 1887 edition of the National Tribune. Pressed into mail duty in 1862, Morris narrowly escaped capture while delivering orders from General Don Carlos Buell directing his men to assemble at Chattanooga. Upon reporting back to Buell, the general—who knew how hazardous the journey would be—replied frankly, "Well, Morris, I never expected to see you again."

This service in the Army of the Cumberland was performed by private soldiers detailed for that purpose. Usually two men were stationed at the headquarters of each division, and it was their duty to see that the mail was promptly transported to and from the division and the nearest railroad communication, however near or remote. The distance varied from a few hundred yards, as at Murfreesboro and Chattanooga, to thirty or forty miles during the Stone River, Chickamauga and Atlanta campaigns. Soldiers detailed for this duty were usually regarded by their comrades as having a "soft thing," but the work was often laborious and full of danger. Guerrillas, bushwhackers, and even apparently inoffensive citizens were always ready to waylay the lonely carrier of Uncle Sam's mail-sack.

At the nearest distributing office the mail for each division was put up in separate sacks and plainly marked with the name of the division commander. These were then sent as near the front as possible by rail. The trains were met by the division mail carrier—in an ambulance until the army crossed the Tennessee River and afterward on horseback—and the mail taken to division headquarters. There it was sorted and put into brigade sacks, which were taken by carriers to their respective brigades, and there distributed into regimental packages and taken by the regimental carrier to each regiment and then sent to the different companies, and finally distributed to the men.

I presume none of us have forgotten what an important event was the arrival of the mail in camp; how eagerly we gathered about the Captain's tent while the names were being called, and the feeling of pleasure or of disappointment as we received or failed to receive the expected missive from loved ones away up in "God's Country."

SERGEANT DANIEL ELDREDGE
3D NEW HAMPSHIRE INFANTRY

While recuperating from a wound he received at Fort Wagner, near Charleston, S.C., Sergeant Eldredge performed his clerical duties so well that he was promoted to second lieutenant. His initiative also extended to financial matters; he made extra money reselling goods and rations, and by charging to ghostwrite letters for the men in his unit. His bookish nature served him well, for at Petersburg his life was saved when a volume in his breast pocket deflected a bullet.

I began during the winter months to write letters for my comrades, the number of which increased with such rapidity that I felt obliged to charge five cents apiece for them: ten cents if I furnished stationery and stamps. From that time until the summer of '63 I had an average of six men to write for, besides my personal correspondence which was not small of itself as I frequently received five or six letters at a time. There were many men in the army who would rather pay twenty five cents for a letter than to write it themselves; some because they lack the faculty and others because they were too lazy. Those whom I wrote for generally handed the newly received letter to me as soon as read, saying "answer that, Eldredge, when you have time" and pass on. In a few days the salutation would be "Answered that letter Eldredge?" Certainly, I would say, here's your old letter with date of receipt and reply endorsed on the back: "Here's your (five or) ten cents" would be the reply or "charge it: I'll pay you next payday." Thus the reader will perceive that although I was a private, I had other sources of revenue than my monthly pay from my Uncle Samuel, and had I been as economical as some others I should at the moment of writing this be worth three or four thousand dollars, whereas I spent my money freely for whatever I desired to make me comfortable internally and externally and am in consequence worth only—well no matter now.

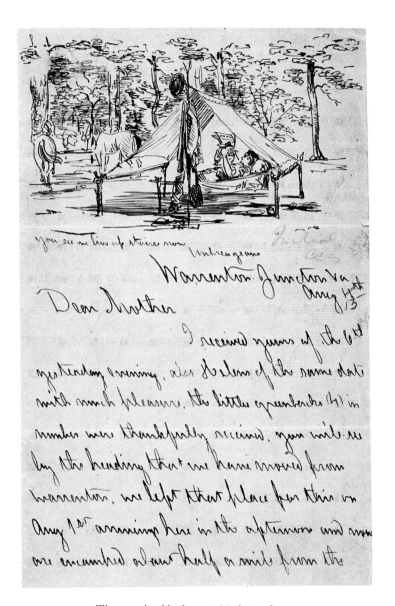

Chief Trumpeter Charles W. Reed spent nearly three years in the 9th Massachusetts Light Artillery as a bugler and topographical engineer. At Gettysburg, his first battle, he risked his life to rescue his commanding officer and was awarded the Medal of Honor. His letters home, a sample of which are shown at right, are filled with sketches that depict the everyday activities of a soldier.

The scene in this August 1862 letter shows the 9th Massachusetts bivouacked near Warrenton Junction, Virginia.

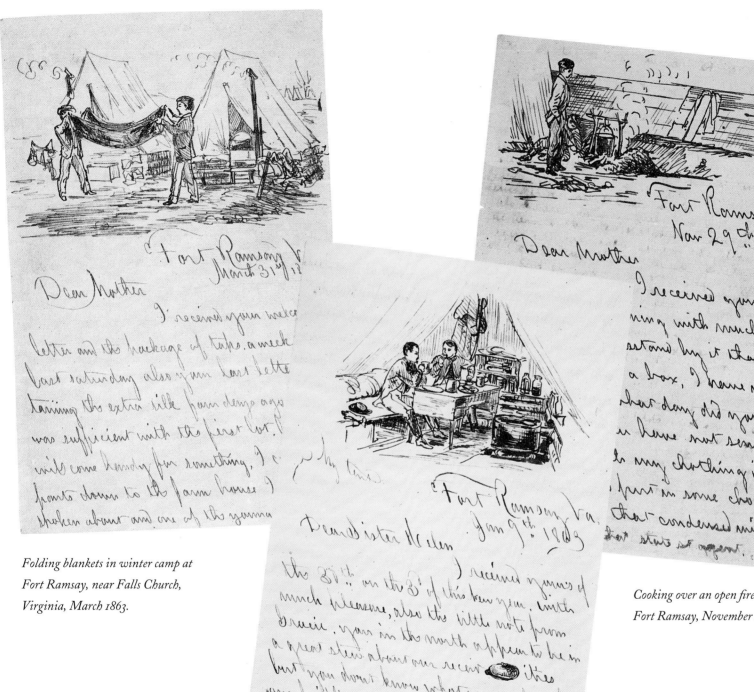

Folding blankets in winter camp at Fort Ramsay, near Falls Church, Virginia, March 1863.

Cooking over an open fire at Fort Ramsay, November 1862.

Eating a meal at Fort Ramsay, January 1863.

SURGEON DANIEL M. HOLT
121ST NEW YORK INFANTRY

Daniel Holt was already 42 years old and a successful physician when he signed up with the 121st New York. He was captured at Chancellorsville in 1863 but was quickly released under an exchange of medical personnel ordered by Robert E. Lee. During the war he contracted tuberculosis, which killed him in 1868.

Camp of the 121st Regiment.
N.Y. Vols White Oak Church, Va.,
March 7th, 1863
My dear Wife:—

Last night I received one of those old fashioned soul inspiring letters from home. Sometimes I think I am growing childish as well as old when I find that I am so easily affected by a kind word. It is so seldom we hear them here, that when they *do* come, it seems like breathings from the spirit land—voices from the other side of the river where our loved ones have gone before and are waiting our arrival. Let them come. It makes us no worse and perhaps much better. I am firmly of the opinion that were more of such letters written to desponding soldiers, we should have less desertion and harder fighting. No man can discharge his duty so cheerfully and promptly when cries of distress and mournful regrets at leaving are constantly poured into his ears, as he can when the partner of his life and object of his affections stirs him up to action by words of patriotic fire and christian enthusiasm. No, it is only those who are the recipients of complaining, fault-finding letters—letters worthy of no virtuous Christian mind—letters such as harrow up all the ill nature within us, and *those who receive no letters,* who are found in the rear when a battle is raging—who can see no beauty in our government—no benefits resulting from its administration and who are ready at all times to despond and talk evil when success does not

attend every movement—it is this class of men, who made unhappy by home influence, is sure to turn away and disgracefully leave our country in the hands of traitors, while the loyal brother fights the battle of both. Then give me such letters as make me feel that I am a man and have a country and family to defend, and gives me an idea of freedom such as God intends all to possess.

CORPORAL TALIAFERRO N. SIMPSON
3D SOUTH CAROLINA INFANTRY

Three of Simpson's cousins were members of the 3d South Carolina. At Antietam one was wounded, one was captured, and one was missing in action; Simpson ventured back onto the battlefield to search in vain for him. Through these hardships he wrote compulsively to his family. Though he was clearly exasperated with the lack of mail he got in return, its absence resulted not from indifference on the part of his family but rather from sporadic mail delivery.

Ask yourselves the question whether it be natural for those at home to treat an absent member as you all have at certain times, and are still treating me, and you will most assuredly acknowledge that my meaning is quite evident.

When Lewis arrived, he gave me a letter from Pa and Ma. For many, many weeks before I had looked in vain for a note of some kind. And since the arrival of Harry, not a line have I received from home. Why is this? Are you getting tired of writing, is paper getting scarce and dear, or are you all getting too lazy to postpone doing nothing to write me a few lines saying that all are well and expressing some affection for your absent boy and buddie? The mail comes regularly every day. None for me. Others can read letters from home. I can't. Why? Simply because you won't write to me. I always supposed that it was natural for a family to have a care for one of its members, whether absent or present. And when that care is lost or gone, I think nature is deviating from its usual path. You think the same, I know, without asking you.

What excuse therefore have you to offer for your conduct? What excuse can you give for this violation of the natural laws by which not only man but every animal in the universal world is governed? When you write I will expect a full explanation and a positive affirmation that such a course will not be pursued in future.

"It seems like breathings from the spirit land—voices from the other side of the river where our loved ones have gone before and are waiting our arrival."

Civil War letters varied in appearance. Perhaps lacking stationery, a relative of Major William B. Clement of the 10th Virginia Cavalry fashioned the envelope above from a scrap of wallpaper. The letter at right, adorned with the hopeful image of a soldier returning home, was sent to Medal of Honor winner George Galloway of the 95th Pennsylvania while he was stationed in Virginia. At top right is a letter to Colonel William Breckinridge of the 9th Kentucky Cavalry.

LIEUTENANT JOHN V. HADLEY
7TH INDIANA INFANTRY

Many members of the 7th Indiana were forsaken by women they left behind, and Lieutenant Hadley grew worried that his love, Mary Jane Hill, was about to do the same. But Mary put his fears to rest in her reply to this letter, and the two were married in 1865. During the war Hadley was wounded twice. Captured, he escaped from a prisoner of war camp. After the war he became a lawyer and served on the Indiana Supreme Court.

Alexandria Va July 22d/62
Miss Mollie J. Hill
Friend Mary—I write you to day under very embarrassing circumstances. For a long time I have been hearing that the channel of your affections was running in an opposite direction—that you were about to adopt another name &c and I never gave it the least attention until very recently. But the unaccountable delay of your letters has forced some suspicion at last. If you have found another more worthy or who has a greater claim upon your affections I am glad for I must say that I never felt myself worthy of that heart which knows no

sentiment that is not pure & holy & which feels no motive but to make happy and blessed all associates.

Hearing what I have heard it is a natural and just desire of mine to be made acquainted with the fact, for if I am writing to a lady whose heart and hand belongs to another, the tenor of my letters is neither polite nor wise. You can, of course recognize their impropriety as well as I. If the report adjudges you rightly, Mary, you will do me at least one more kindness & write me at once, frankly about the matter, that I may not labor under misapprehensions. For if I have ever been confidential and faithful to you, I shall ever remain so to be and confide evrything that you may see proper to divulge. Let me know the worst and if the report be true let the cords of intimacy be a little relaxed but I hope those of friendship may never be broken.

I cannot write longer—politeness forbids—I could tell you many things but cannot now for this is the third letter at least since I had one from you. excuse my impertinence for you know my honesty.

I am as ever Jno

Portable writing kits, which contained pen, ink, and paper and rolled up for easy storage, found wide use during the war. The kit at right belonged to Sergeant Henry S. Parmalee of the 1st Connecticut Cavalry. Parmalee, a former piano maker, lost his writing hand after being shot near Petersburg in 1865.

"Oh god how proud I feel of you just to think that my wife was tested and remained true."

PRIVATE JOHN D. TIMERMAN
3D NEW YORK CAVALRY

Timerman enlisted after an argument with his wife, Mary, thinking the war would be over in a matter of months. He ended up spending more than three years in the Union army, was captured twice, and survived a stint in Richmond's Libby Prison. Despite their disagreements John loved and missed his wife and was outraged to hear that one Henry Dupler had made advances on Mary in his absence. There is no record of how Timerman settled his "debt" with Dupler.

Camp Bates Dec 15 1861
Dear Wife
I was quite Surprised to hear Such news from Henry Dupler but I hope the time will come when he will have to meet me and then I think I will Settle my Debt that I owe him in regard to his insulting you and I think I will make him chaw his words or he make his words gospel. but never mind it at present but one thing certain I am going to come to See you next pay day if I have to desert But Oh my dear how happy I am that you did not give in to his wishes for what would have been my feelings if I should have heard to the contrary but enough of that I always thought I had as true a wife as there was living but now I know it and oh god how proud I feel of you just to think that my wife was tested and remained true to her Dear husband but perhaps Some would Say he will never know it is true I might never have found out but what would have been your feeling if ever you Should have layed in my arms and then think that you had deceived me or what would have been your feelings Supposing you should have heard that I had broken my oath and deserted you by giving that to others that I most Solumly Swor Should be yours. . . .

    From Your True & Effectionate Husband
    JD Timerman
    P.S. Write soon
    Bless you

Mary Timerman posed for this photograph in her "young married days" while her husband was at war. After his return, they spent an additional 31 years together.

CORPORAL GEORGE S. RICHARDSON
6TH IOWA INFANTRY

The Midwest was a stronghold of the so-called Copperheads—Northerners who opposed the war and the policies of President Lincoln. But they were universally reviled by soldiers such as George Richardson, who felt the Copperheads were undermining their military efforts as well as giving their home states a bad name. About the same time Richardson penned this letter to his family, his brother, William, also a member of Company G, sent one expressing his hope that his regiment "be recalled long enough to wipe out the traitors."

Camp 6th Iowa Infantry
Oak Ridge, Mississippi
August 9th, 1863
Dear Father and Mother,

I have just received your letter of the 22d of July and hasten to answer it although I had not intended to do so for I wrote about two days ago, but for once in my life I write from the impulse of the moment.

I have just read in a northern paper that you have had trouble in your vicinity with the most cowardly and insignificant enemy that our common country has been disgraced with, i.e., the Copperheads. Before this reaches you perhaps they will have done their worst. There are some who will still be neutral and are they to go unpunished? Are they going to hurrah for Jeff Davis within hearing of our homes when we are here fighting for our common country? Are these cowards to be allowed such privileges and not get what they justly merit? Are you too weak to help yourselves or are you going to rise as one man and drive the cursed traitors from your midst?

Here we are on the point of achieving what we have worked for two years to accomplish! We had thought that there were enough loyal men in Iowa to keep down traitors. We have even boasted over the soldiers of other states in this one thing, but now they can throw it in our teeth that Iowa too is disloyal.

Dad, I am in sober earnest when I say now that you must be careful. Don't waiver in your devotion to our glorious country. Don't let them betray you by smiles or promises. Load your gun and strike the traitor before you have to sacrifice one atom of principle. Do they call you an abolitionist? That is no disgrace now. Every true union man is for the union, the government and the administration even if we have to not only free the negroes but confiscate the last dollars worth of property belonging to the Rebels. There is one thing more I want you to do while these traitors are in their glory. Watch who the sympathizers are and put their names in black and white so that we can settle with them when we come home if it can not be paid to them before.

You may think that I have been too forward to express my opinion in regard to some persons in your neighborhood. Do you look at the matter as we do, or has the peace and security that you have enjoyed at home damped your patriotism? Are you tired of the war because it is taking a few paltry dollars from your purse to pay taxes or is it possible that you have not the interest that you should have? I hope this is not the case. I ask you, yes it is what every soldier demands of friends at home, to let your light so shine that others may profit by it and that traitors may have nothing to encourage them in their hellish designs.

It is getting quite dark so I will close. We are both quite well. Write soon as you can.

Your affectionate Son,
Geo. S. Richardson

"Load your gun and strike the traitor before you have to sacrifice one atom of principle."

PRIVATE MADISON KILPATRICK
5TH GEORGIA MILITIA REGIMENT

Aware that his case of rheumatism would not get him the discharge he needed to oversee the family farm—the condition did not rate medical attention—Private Kilpatrick advised his wife by letter on how to manage the farm. And since it was impossible for Mrs. Kilpatrick and her sons to do all the work themselves, they had to be sure none of their slaves escaped or were executed by Confederate patrols that roamed the Georgia countryside in search of runaways.

August 12, 1864

Dear Dear Wife,

I received your letters yesterday and you can have no idea how welcome they were for there is nothing in this wide world that I care anything for like I do your love and the love of my children. I am glad to hear that our losses were no greater. Tell the negroes to stay at home and not be led into any difficulty for there will apt to be hanging done. If the negroes are unruly tell them I have been a good master, have waited on and cared for them when sick and now they must fight for you and the children if necessary. Give them more meat than you have been giving them—have the stock all looked after if the Yankees should return let the negroes take the stock and separate and stay in the old fields—and not have them all together for we might lose them all—Be sure to tell the negroes to stay at home of nights—for they might be hung for being in bad company. Sow turnips, lots of them. Tell Anthony to clear the bottom from where the grind stone was lost to the head field fence—burn the logs. Cut down saplings—kill the large trees—break up twice and sow turnips, then go over with hoes

and kill all the grass—the turnips can be sowed broad cast—you had best shear the sheep right now—get the rams I left word for you to get—Fodder will have to be saved soon let all the negroes pull fodder for awhile for I did not save enough last year—but if you want some of them to help about the wool take as many as you want—If John is discharged he can have plenty of fodder pulled with few hands—I should have the sugar cane worked for it will be of great service to us—if you cannot get the bottom cleared in time for the fodder omit it but we will need the turnips for the sheep and should have them if we can. There is no chance for me to be discharged—they do not even doctor rhumatic men up here.

EMILY WATERS
ROSELAND PLANTATION, LOUISIANA

Although they were free at the war's end, Southern blacks still faced harassment from their ex-masters. One of the most common tactics, used on ex-slave Emily Waters, was for plantation owners to evict former slaves unless they paid high rents. A sympathetic Union officer granted Waters' soldier-husband leave to resolve the matter; he arrived home in time to find a provost guard about to expel his family.

Roseland Plantation July 16th 1865

My Dear Husband I received a letter from you a week before last and was glad to hear that you were well and happy. This is the fifth letter I have written you and I have received only

"My Children which I once thought troublesome. would now be a great delight to me even when they are most mischevious."

one—Please write as often as you can as I am always anxious to hear from you. I and the children are all well—but I am in a great deal of trouble as Master John Humphries has come home from the Rebel army and taken charge of the place and says he is going to turn us all out on the Levee unless we pay him (8.00) Eight Dollars a month for house rent—Now I have no money of any account and I am not able to get enough to pay so much rent, and I want you to get a furlough as soon as you can and come home and find a place for us to live in. and besides Amelia is very sick and wants you to come home and see her if possible she has been sick with fever now over two weeks and is getting very low—Your mother and all the rest of your folks are well and all send their regards & want to see you as soon as you can manage to come—My mother sends her compliments & hopes to see you soon

My children are going to school, but I find it very hard to feed them all, and if you can not come I hope you will send me something to help me get along

I get all the work I can and am doing the best I can to get along, but if they turn me out I dont know what I shall do—However I will try & keep the children along until you come or send me some assistance

Thank God we are all well, and I hope we may always be so Give my regards to all the boys. Come home as soon as you can, and cherish me as ever

Your Aff wife
Emily Waters

PRIVATE JACOB W. BARTMESS
39TH INDIANA MOUNTED INFANTRY

Being away from home for so long gave Private Bartmess, like so many other soldiers, a renewed appreciation for the simple pleasures of family life. His letters home reflect this, talking frequently of the things he misses. After his return from the war in July of 1865, Bartmess worked as a preacher and had three additional children with his wife, Amanda.

Dec. 23 '62.
Amanda Bartmess
Camp near Nashville Tenn
Amanda—my own dear wife.—.

I have been for the last few days and am at the present quite grunty. my Stomache is out of fix. I went to the doctor this morning and got a dose of oil; may be the oil will Settle it. The brigade went out on drill this morning but I did not go along.

I received your letter of the 11th. and 12th. yesterday evening, which gave me much Satisfaction. I received a letter from you about one week ago stating that you were sick., and O, how anxious every evening when the mail came. since that was I to get a letter from you to hear how you was getting. I am sorry that you was sick but am glad of the change and hope you may get well and stout as you ever have been. You Said that Elliot was very Mischevious. Tell him that papy says he must not be too bad and you may be sure that I would like to be there and take lista on my lap and talk to her and hear her talk. Well my prayer is that the time may soon come.

You say you miss me when you go to bed Ah, dear Wife. When meal time comes. and I sit down on the ground. useing the ground for a table. and having on the table some hard crackers some old bacon. a coffee pot full of coffee, which pot is so black and hard looking that you would scarcely use it for a Slop pot at home, then pour my coffee into an old tin cup which would be a disgrace to the kitchen at home then I miss you. When I lie down on the ground at night with my overcoat for a pillow and my blanket for a cover heareing oath after oath till at last nature yealds and my eyes close in Sleep. O then I miss When I go about camp hearing the continual din of camp. there I miss you. where er'e I go in whatever company I am. I miss my dearest one—my wife.—

And my Children which I once thought troublesome. would now be a great delight to me even when they are most mischevious. I most earnestly pray that these stat of things will not last long. . . .

I would love to have yours and the childrens pictures taken in a double case and sent to me yours on one side and the childrens on the other. but it will cost too much. do just as you like about that. I am sorry to hear that the boys do not get along any better than they do. for I would like to have Harrison with me then I believe I would get along better. Tell the boys to write to me as often as they can. though I have not wrote to them. the letters that I send to you will do for the whole family. I believe I will close this letter. I think I have averaged two letters a week I wish you may do as well we have had nice dry wether here ever since I have been here Amanda I wish I could tell you how deep my affection is for you but I can not so nomore at this time.

J. W. Bartmess.

This photograph of an unidentified Confederate captain and his son was typical of the comforting family pictures that soldiers carried with them during the war.

"I often lay awake in my tent at night, and wander in imagination back to my distant home—I wonder if my dear wife is asleep, or is she up nursing the baby and trying to get him asleep."

PRIVATE SAMUEL A. BURNEY
Infantry Battalion, Cobb's Legion, Georgia Volunteers

Camped near Yorktown, Virginia, just 100 yards from the spot where the British surrendered to George Washington in 1781, Samuel Burney wrote his wife a letter that echoed the sentiments of countless soldiers who left their families behind. Burney spent three and a half years in the Confederate army and was wounded once, but he survived his ordeal and returned home at the war's end.

Camp Washington Yorktown, Va.
Oct 8' 1861 Thursday 11'oclk A.M.
Dearest Wife,

. . . In your letter you wrote the baby had the thrash. I can only repeat the hope expressed in my last, that he may recover speedily. I hope my dear wife that you have had no more attacks of the head-ache. I know how you suffer from them, and I often pray that you may be freed from any further attacks. Oh! how I hope that you are sustained by the Divine arm. It is a support upon which you may repose, and never feel disturbed. Let the Lord be your helper and you shall not faint. Wife, I guess you think that I have much to say in my letters about trusting in God. It is true and I shall continue to speak of it. It is upper-most in my heart, and it is manifested from the mouth, and by the pen. Oh! that God would bless you and comfort you—may you be kept as the apple of the eye, and hid under the shadow of his wing. I pray God that he would be a husband to my wife and a father to my son. I love to trust in God, for I know I shall never be deceived—my reward is as certain as the Eternal Throne.

I think we have had about half dozen days appointed upon which we would leave this place. I can say that we are here, and no more. Cobb knows no more when we will leave, than I do. I will write to you and let it be known after we have moved. This much is true—we expect to leave every day. I know that the little babe is as sweet as ever. I earnestly hope that he is well and I fancy now that I can see his sweet little laughing eyes & his dimpled rosy cheeks. Sometimes I paint him before me asleep—with his little hands seizing each ear —the very quintessence of infant beauty innocence and love. When I think of you & him, and then myself I can but re-commit us all into God's holy hands.

The war will have this good effect I think; it will cause a fresher love for home to spring up in the hearts of many whose dissolute habits forbade their staying there. It will make husbands more attentive, kind & affectionate. It will humble the proud, and be a source of benefit to all those who feel the chastening hand of God. How do you get on at night with the baby; I often lay awake in my tent at night, and wander in imagination back to my distant home—I wonder if my dear wife is asleep, or is she up nursing the baby and trying to get him asleep—The baby is one month old now; I guess he has changed his looks some. I recollect how he looked, exactly, when I left you and him. You will soon be able to walk about the yard if not already. You must go up and see our family when you get strength enough. I know that they all love you as they do me. My dear Mother I know feels so tenderly to you as the Mother that bore you; She will exhaust her energies in ministering to your comfort. If you need anything you must send and get it; while I do not believe in excess in anything, I believe that God has given us what we have, richly to enjoy while we may.

A Union soldier at Rappahannock Station,
Virginia, loses himself in a hometown newspaper
in this 1864 Edwin Forbes study.

GLOSSARY

adjutant—A staff officer assisting the commanding officer, usually with correspondence.

A tent—A canvas tent whose sloping sides form the letter *A*. Designed for four men but often housed more.

battery—The basic unit of artillery, consisting of four to six guns.

bee gum hat—A broad-brimmed slouch hat with a conical crown resembling a bee gum, or hive.

bog-trotter—A slang term for someone of Irish descent.

bounty—A monetary incentive given to induce men to enlist. A bounty jumper was a soldier who took a bounty upon enlisting and then deserted.

coffee cooler—A shirker or malingerer. One who will begin work "when the coffee cools."

"commissary"—A kind of whiskey issued by the army's commissary department.

Copperhead—A Northern Democrat favoring a negotiated peace.

cush—To Southern soldiers, virtually any edible concoction using cornmeal or corn bread as a base. The cornmeal could be fried in bacon fat, stewed with meat or other ingredients, or otherwise prepared.

fatigue duty—A general term for any manual or menial work done by soldiers.

forage—To search for and acquire provisions from nonmilitary sources. To soldiers of the Civil War it often meant, simply, stealing.

furlough—A leave of absence granted to a soldier.

gum blanket—A waterproof blanket, treated with rubber and often in poncho form.

hardtack—A durable cracker, or biscuit, made of plain flour and water and normally about three inches square and a half-inch thick.

haversack—A shoulder bag, usually strapped over the right shoulder to rest on the left hip, for carrying personal items and rations.

John Barleycorn—A slang term for whiskey.

mess—A group of soldiers who prepare and eat meals together, or to eat such a meal; the place where such a meal is prepared and eaten.

muster—To assemble. To be mustered in is to be enlisted or enrolled in service. To be mustered out is to be discharged from service, usually on expiration of a set time.

order arms—The position for holding a shoulder arm in which the weapon, with its butt resting on the ground, is held vertically along the soldier's right side.

orderly—A soldier assigned to a superior officer for various duties, such as carrying messages.

pard—Short for partner, implying an especially close friendship.

parole—The pledge of a soldier released after being captured by the enemy that he will not take up arms again until he has been properly exchanged.

pas de charge—The official name for the drumbeat ordering a charge.

phonography—A system of phonetic writing devised by Isaac Pitman in 1837.

picket—One or more soldiers on guard to protect the larger unit from surprise attack.

provost guard—A detail of soldiers acting as police under the supervision of an officer called a provost marshal.

ration—A specified allotment of food for one person (or animal) per day. The amounts and nature of rations varied by time and place throughout the war. Rations may also refer simply to any food provided by the army.

red eye—A slang term for strong alcoholic beverages.

rifle—Any weapon with spiral grooves cut into the bore, which give spin to the projectile, adding range and accuracy. Usually applied to cannon or weapons fired from the shoulder.

secesh—A slang term for secessionist.

see the elephant—To participate in combat.

shelter tent—Also called a *tente d'abri*, pup tent, or dog tent, it consists of two shelter halves (each carried by a single soldier) buttoned together and hung over a ridgepole.

Sibley tent—Tent that resembled the tipi of the Plains Indians; named for its inventor, Confederate general Henry Hopkins Sibley. Conical, erected on a tripod, with a smoke hole at the top, the tent could easily accommodate 12 men and their equipment.

sperm candle—A candle made from the fatty substance spermaceti, harvested from sperm whales.

spoon—To lie down, under crowded conditions, on one's side with knees drawn up, belly against the back of another and back against another's belly, like spoons in a stack.

stack arms—To set aside weapons, usually three or more in a pyramid, interlocking at the end of the barrel with the butts on the ground.

sutler—A peddler with a permit to remain with troops in camp or in the field and sell food, drink, and other supplies.

tattoo—Drum or bugle call signaling the time to return to quarters in the evening. Taps, initiated in 1862, calls for lights out.

toadstickers—A slang term for an officer's sword or a large knife of any kind.

turnspit—Formerly a small mongrel dog used on a treadmill to turn a spit. An unqualified and incapable person.

ACKNOWLEDGMENTS

The editors wish to thank the following for their valuable assistance in the preparation of this volume:
John Ahladas, Museum of the Confederacy, Richmond; Paul Bascom, Chesapeake, Va.; Arthur W. Bergeron Jr., Baton Rouge, La.; William I. Erwin Jr., Duke University, Durham, N.C.; Ann Frantillo, Bentley Historical Library, Ann Arbor, Mich.; Randy W. Hackenburg, U.S. Army Military History Institute, Carlisle Barracks, Pa.; Corinne Hudgins, The Museum of the Confederacy, Richmond; Henry D. Jamison III, Brentwood, Tenn.; Larry Jones, Austin, Tex.; Jenny Kane, Cleveland Health Sciences Library, Cleveland; Carol Mathias, Archives, Nicholls State University, Thibodaux, La.; Elizabeth Whitley Roberson, Williamston, N.C.; Bobby Roberts, Central Arkansas Library System, Little Rock; Carolyn Smith, Fauquier County Library, Warrenton, Va.; Sherry Wilding-White, New Hampshire Historical Society, Concord; Michael J. Winney, U.S. Army Military History Institute, Carlisle Barracks, Pa.; Mrs. Bette Wurzlow, Shriever, La.; Roberta Zonghi, Rare Books Division, Boston Public Library, Boston.

PICTURE CREDITS

The sources for the illustrations are listed below. Credits from left to right are separated by semicolons, from top to bottom by dashes. All calligraphy by Mary Lou O'Brian/Inkwell, Inc. Dust jacket: front, National Archives; rear, from *The Papers of Randolph Abbott Shotwell*, Vol. 1, edited by J. G. de Roulhac Hamilton, North Carolina Historical Commission, Raleigh, N.C., 1929, copied by Philip Brandt George. 6, 7: Art by Paul Salmon. 8: Florida Photographic Collection. 12: Cooper-Hewitt, National Design Museum, Smithsonian Institution/Art Resource, N.Y. 14, 15: Courtesy of the Burton Historical Collection, Detroit Public Library, copied by Tom Sherry; inset, Illinois State Historical Society. 16: From *Yankee in Gray: The Civil War Memoirs of Henry E. Handerson*, introduction by Clyde Lottridge Cummer, The Press of The Western Reserve University, 1962, courtesy Cleveland Health Sciences Library, copied by Philip Brandt George; Confederate Memorial Museum, New Orleans, La., from *Portraits of Conflict: A Photographic History of Louisiana in the Civil War*, by Carl Moneyhon and Bobby Roberts, University of Arkansas Press, Fayetteville, 1990, copied by Philip Brandt George. 17: Frances H. Rainey; General Sweeney's Museum, Republic, Mo. 18: Courtesy of Paul Bascom, from *Dear Lizzie*, © 1978 by Elizabeth Parker Bascom, copied by Philip Brandt George. 20: Frank and Marie-Thérèse Wood Print Collections, Alexandria, Va.; inset, State Historical Society of Wisconsin. 21: Howard Michael Madaus Collection, photographed by Leo Johnson. 22: Hargrett Rare Book and Manuscript Library, University of Georgia Libraries; Henry D. Jamison III. 23: From *Well Mary: Civil War Letters of a Wisconsin Volunteer*, edited by Margaret Brobst Roth, University of Wisconsin Press, Madison, 1994, courtesy Margaret Brobst Roth, copied by Philip Brandt George. 24, 25: Chicago Historical Society No. iCHi-19841; from *Meade's Headquarters, 1863–1865: Letters of Colonel Theodore Lyman from the Wilderness to Appomattox*, edited by George R. Agassiz, Atlantic Monthly Press, Boston, 1922, copied by Philip Brandt George. 26: Library of Congress. 28: Museum of the Confederacy, Richmond, Va., photographed by Katherine Wetzel. 29, 30: The Western Reserve Historical Society, Cleveland. 31: Courtesy Stamatelos Brothers Collection, Cambridge, Mass., photographed by Andrew K. Howard. 32: Courtesy T. Scott Sanders. 33: From *The Rough Side of War*, edited with biographical sketch by Arnold Gates, The Basin Publishing Co., Garden City, N.Y., 1987; courtesy Doug Bast/Boonsborough Museum of History, photographed by Larry Sherer (5). 34: Courtesy Doug Bast/Boonsborough Museum of History, photographed by Larry Sherer. 35: Library of Congress Neg. No. B818-10032. 37: Library of Congress Neg. No. BN8255-91. 38: Ed and Maureen Simpson. 39: Special Collections Library, Duke University, Durham, N.C., photographed by George S. Cook, Charleston, S.C. 40, 41: From *War from the Inside*, by Frederick L. Hitchcock, Press of J. B. Lippincott Co., Philadelphia, 1904, copied by Philip Brandt George; Library of Congress. 43: Library of Congress. 44: Courtesy Special Collections, James Graham Leyburn Library, Washington & Lee University, Lexington, Va. 45: Courtesy Stamatelos Brothers Collection, Cambridge, Mass., photographed by Andrew K. Howard. 46: The Western Reserve Historical Society, Cleveland—from *The Guns of '62*, Vol. 2 of *The Image of War, 1861–1865*, The National Historical Society, Doubleday & Co., Inc., Garden City, N.Y., 1982, courtesy Blackdog & Leventhal Publishers, copied by Philip Brandt George. 47: Museum of the Confederacy, Richmond, Va., photographed by Larry Sherer. 48: Confederate Calendar Works, courtesy Larry Jones. 49: U.S. Army Military History Institute (USAMHI), Carlisle Barracks, Pa., copied by A. Pierce Bounds. 50: Library of Congress. 51: Library of Congress, Gilbert Thompson Papers. 52: Bill Turner. 53: Courtesy Adele Mitchell, Carlisle, Pa., copied by A. Pierce Bounds. 54: USAMHI, Carlisle Barracks, Pa., copied by A. Pierce Bounds. 56: Nelsonian Institute, photographed by Larry Sherer. 58: From *The Papers of Randolph Abbott Shotwell*, Vol. 1, edited by J. G. de Roulhac Hamilton, North Carolina Historical Commission, Raleigh, N.C., 1929, copied by Philip Brandt George. 59: From *Hardtack and Coffee, or The Unwritten Story of Army Life*, by John D. Billings, George M. Smith & Co., Boston, 1888, copied by Philip Brandt George. 62, 63: From *Ham Chamberlayne—Virginian, Letters and Papers of an Artillery Officer in the War for Southern Independence, 1861–1865*, edited by C. G. Chamberlayne, Press of the Dietz Printing Co., Richmond, Va., 1932, copied by Larry Sherer; from *Weep Not for Me, Dear Mother*, by Elizabeth Whitley Roberson, © 1991, used by permission of the publisher, Pelican Co., Inc. (2) 64: Courtesy Chris Nelson. 65: Library of Congress Neg. No. 26543. 66: Courtesy Dave Zullo, photographed by Evan H. Sheppard. 67: USAMHI, Carlisle Barracks, Pa., copied by A. Pierce Bounds. 68: From *Reminiscences of a Private: William E. Bevens of the First Arkansas Infantry, C.S.A.*, edited with an introduction by Daniel E. Sutherland, University of Arkansas Press, Fayetteville, 1992, copied by Philip Brandt George. 69: From *The Photographic History of the Civil War*, Vol. 7, edited by Holland Thompson, Ph.D., The Review of Reviews Co., 1911, copied by Philip Brandt George. 70: Massachusetts Commandery of the Military Order of the Loyal Legion of the United States and the U.S. Army Military History Institute (MASS-MOLLUS/USAMHI), copied by A. Pierce Bounds. 71: Library of Congress. 72: From *The Mail Goes Through, or The Civil War Letters of George Drake (1846–1918)*, edited by Julia A. Drake, Anchor Publishing Co., San Angelo, Tex., 1964, copied by Philip Brandt George. 73: Courtesy Tom Farish, photographed by Michael Latil. 74: New Hampshire Historical Society No. F4390—courtesy Doug Bast/Boonsborough Museum of History, photographed by Larry Sherer. 75: Museum of the Confederacy, Richmond, Va., photographed by Larry Sherer (2); Herb Peck Jr. 77: Library of Congress. 78: Photo by E & HT Anthony & Co., New York, Minnesota Historical Society. 80: Museum of the Confederacy, Richmond, Va., photographed by Larry Sherer. 81: Hayes Presidential Center, Freemont, Ohio. 82: Courtesy Collection of C. Paul Loane, photographed by Larry Sherer. 84: Florida State Archives, Neg. No. 2503. 85: From *"Dear Friends": The Civil War Letters and Diary of Charles Edwin Cort*, compiled and edited with commentaries by Helyn W. Tomlinson, 1962, copied by Philip Brandt George—Museum of the Confederacy, Richmond, Va., photographed by Larry Sherer. 86, 87: USAMHI, Carlisle Barracks, Pa., copied by A. Pierce Bounds. 88: The Western Reserve Historical Society, Cleveland—courtesy Don Troiani Collection, photographed by Larry Sherer. 90, 91: The Western Reserve Historical Society, Cleveland. 92, 93: Library of Congress. 94: From *The History of the Tenth Massachusetts Battery of Light Artillery in the War of the Rebellion, 1862-1865*, by John D. Billings, Arakelyan Press, Boston, 1909, copied by Philip Brandt George; Museum of the Confederacy, Richmond, Va., photographed by Larry Sherer (2). 95: Library of Congress; L. M. Strayer Collection, photographed by Bill Patterson (2). 96: Photo by Illingworth, Minnesota Historical Society—Eleanor S. Brockenbrough Library, Museum of the Confederacy, Richmond, Va., photographed by Katherine Wetzel. 97: Museum of the Confederacy, Richmond, Va., photographed by Larry Sherer—courtesy Will Gorges, New Bern, N.C., photographed by Larry Sherer. 98: USAMHI, Carlisle Barracks, Pa., copied by A. Pierce Bounds. 99: Austin History Center, Austin Public Library; Library of Congress. 100: From *The Guns of '62*, Vol. 2 of *The Image of War, 1861-1865*, National Historical Society, Doubleday & Co., Inc., Garden City, N.Y., 1982, courtesy George Eastman House, Rochester, N.Y., copied by Philip Brandt George. 101: Library of Congress. 102, 103: Library of Congress— Museum of the Confederacy, Richmond, Va., photographed by Katherine Wetzel. 104, 105: Courtesy L. M. Strayer Collection, photographed by Bill Patterson (2); Library of Congress. 107: Courtesy L. M. Strayer Collection, photographed by Bill Patterson; from *Four Years*

on the Firing Line, by James Cooper Nisbet, McCowat-Mercer Press, Inc., Jackson, Tenn., 1963, copied by Philip Brandt George. 109: State Museum of Pennsylvania, Pennsylvania Historical and Museum Commission (2); Frank & Marie-Thérèse Wood Print Collections, Alexandria, Va. 110, 111: From *The Guns of '62,* Vol. 2 of *The Image of War, 1861-1865*, The National Historical Society, Doubleday & Co., Inc., Garden City, N.Y., 1982, courtesy Blackdog & Leventhal Publishers, copied by Philip Brandt George—courtesy Les Jensen, photographed by Philip Brandt George. 112: Courtesy Doug Bast/Boonsborough Museum of History, photographed by Larry Sherer; courtesy Dave Zullo, photographed by Evan H. Sheppard (2). 113: Reprinted by permission of Alec Thomas, from *Gone for a Soldier: The Civil War Memoirs of Private Alfred Bellard*, edited by David Herbert Donald, published by Little, Brown and Co., Boston, 1975, copied by Philip Brandt George. 114: Library of Congress. 115: Courtesy Dave Zullo. 116: Historic Thibodaux Collection, Allen J. Ellender Archives, Nicholls State University, Thibodaux, La. 117: From *How Soldiers Were Made, or The War as I Saw It*, by B. F. Scribner, published by Donohue & Henneberry, Printers and Binders, New Albany, Ind., 1887, copied by Philip Brandt George. 118, 119: Library of Congress. 120: Courtesy of the Civil War Library and Museum, Philadelphia, Pa. 19103, copied by Blake A. Magner. 122: Museum of the Confederacy, Richmond, Va., photographed by Larry Sherer. 123: Eleanor S. Brockenbrough Library, The Museum of the Confederacy, Richmond, Va., photographed by Katherine Wetzel. 124, 125: From *Portraits of Conflict: A Photographic History of Mississippi in the Civil War*, by Bobby Roberts and Carl Moneyhon, University of Arkansas Press, Fayetteville, 1990, courtesy Mississippi Department of Archives and History— Library of Congress. 126, 127: Library of Congress. 128: Bently Historical Library, University of Michigan, Ann Arbor. 129: Courtesy Doug Bast/Boonsborough Museum of History, photographed by Larry Sherer. 130, 131: Courtesy Caroline J. Pardee's Collection, Akron, Ohio, from *My Dear Carrie: The Civil War Letters of George K. Pardee and Family*, edited by Robert H. Jones with Caroline J. Pardee, Summit County Historical Society Press, 1994,

copied by Philip Brandt George (2); Special Collections (Orlando Poe Collection), U.S. Military Academy Library, West Point, N.Y., copied by Henry Groskinsky. 132: From *The Story of a Confederate Boy in the Civil War*, by David E. Johnston, Glass & Prudhomme Co., Portland, Oreg., 1845. 133: From *Detailed Minutiae of Soldier Life in the Army of Northern Virginia, 1861-1865*, by Carlton McCarthy, The Riverside Press, Cambridge, Mass., 1882, copied by Philip Brandt George. 134: Frances H. Evans, Tupelo, Miss. 135: From *A Confederate Surgeon's Letters to His Wife*, by Spencer Glasgow Welch, The Continental Book Co., Marietta, Ga., 1954, copied by Philip Brandt George. 136: Lance J. Herdegen. 138: From *Detailed Minutiae of Soldier Life in the Army of Northern Virginia, 1861-1865*, by Carlton McCarthy, The Riverside Press, Cambridge, Mass., 1882, copied by Philip Brandt George. 140: Special Collections (Orlando Poe Collection), U.S. Military Academy Library, West Point, N.Y., copied by Henry Groskinsky. 141: From *Sad Earth, Sweet Heaven: The Diary of Lucy Rebecca Buck*, 2d ed., edited by Dr. William P. Buck, Buck Publishing Co., Birmingham, Ala., 1992, copied by Philip Brandt George; Library of Congress. 142: Courtesy Doug Bast/Boonsborough Museum of History, photographed by Larry Sherer. 143: Reprinted by permission of Alec Thomas. 144: Library of Congress. 145: From *A Civil War Courtship: The Letters of Edwin Weller from Antietam to Atlanta*, edited by William Walton, Doubleday & Co., Inc., Garden City, N.Y., 1980, copied by Philip Brandt George. 146: USAMHI, Carlisle Barracks, Pa. copied by A. Pierce Bounds. 148: Library of Congress; Library of Congress Neg. No. 603486. 149: Library of Congress. 150: USAMHI, Carlisle Barracks, Pa., copied by A. Pierce Bounds. 151: National Postal Museum, Smithsonian Institution (2)—courtesy Dave Zullo, photographed by Evan H. Sheppard. 152: Courtesy Stamatelos Brothers Collection, Cambridge, Mass., photographed by Larry Sherer. 153: Tara Ann Blazer and Alice S. Cook. 154: From *"For My Country": The Richardson Letters, 1861-1865*, compiled and edited by Gordon C. Jones, Broadfoot Publishing Co., Wendell, N.C., 1984, copied by Philip Brandt George. 157: From *Still More Confederate Faces*, by D. Serrano, Metropolitan Co., N.Y. 159: Library of Congress.

BIBLIOGRAPHY

BOOKS

Anderson, John Q., ed. *Campaigning with Parsons' Texas Cavalry Brigade, CSA: The War Journals and Letters of the Four Orr Brothers, 12th Texas Cavalry Regiment.* Hillsboro, Tex.: Hill Junior College, 1967.

Arms and Equipment of the Confederacy (Echoes of Glory series). Alexandria, Va.: Time-Life Books, 1991.

Arms and Equipment of the Union (Echoes of Glory series). Alexandria, Va.: Time-Life Books, 1991.

Barclay, Ted. *Ted Barclay, Liberty Hall Volunteers: Letters from the Stonewall Brigade (1861-1864).* Berryville, Va.: Rockbridge Publishing, 1992.

Beaudot, William J. K., and Lance J. Herdegen. *An Irishman in the Iron Brigade: The Civil War Memoirs of James P. Sullivan, Sergt., Company K, 6th Wisconsin Volunteers.* Bronx, N.Y.: Fordham University Press, 1993.

Bellard, Alfred. *Gone for a Soldier: The Civil War Memoirs of Private Alfred Bellard.* Ed. by David Herbert Donald. Boston: Little, Brown, 1975.

Bevens, William E. *Reminiscences of a Private: William E. Bevens of the First Arkansas Infantry, C. S. A.* Ed. by Daniel E. Sutherland. Fayetteville: University of Arkansas Press, 1992.

Billings, John D. *Hardtack and Coffee, or The Unwritten Story of Army Life.* Boston: George M. Smith, 1888.

Bircher, William. *A Drummer-Boy's Diary: Comprising Four Years of Service with the Second Regiment Minnesota Veteran Volunteers, 1861 to 1865.* Ed. by Newell L. Chester. St. Cloud, Minn.: North Star Press of St. Cloud, 1995 (reprint of 1889 edition).

Blackford, W. W. *War Years with Jeb Stuart.* New York: Charles Scribner's Sons, 1945.

Buck, Lucy Rebecca. *Sad Earth, Sweet Heaven: The Diary of Lucy Rebecca Buck during the War between the States.* Ed. by William P. Buck. Birmingham, Ala.: The Cornerstone, 1973.

Chamberlayne, John Hampden. *Ham Chamberlayne—Virginian: Letters and Papers of an Artillery Officer in the War for Southern Independence, 1861-1865.* Wilmington, N.C.: Broadfoot Publishing, 1992 (reprint of 1932 edition).

Chambers, William Pitt. *Blood & Sacrifice: The Civil War Journal of a Confederate Soldier.* Ed. by Richard A. Baumgartner. Huntington, W.Va.: Blue Acorn Press, 1994.

Cort, Charles Edwin. *"Dear Friends": The Civil War Letters and Diary of Charles Edwin Cort.* Comp. and ed. by Helyn W. Tomlinson. N.p., 1962.

Crawford, James Garvin. *"Dear Lizzie": Letters Written by James "Jimmy" Garvin Crawford to His Sweetheart Martha Elizabeth "Lizzie" Wilson while He Was in the Federal Army during the War between the States, 1862-1865.* Ed. by Elizabeth Ethel Parker Bascom. [Ridgewood, N.J.]: Elizabeth Parker Bascom, 1978.

Davis, Sidney Morris. *Common Soldier Uncommon War: Life as a Cavalryman in the Civil War.* Ed. by Charles F. Cooney. Bethesda, Md.: John H. Davis Jr., 1994.

Davis, William C., and Bell Irvin Wiley, eds. *Photographic History of the Civil War: Fort Sumter to Gettysburg.* New York: Black Dog & Leventhal, 1994.

Dawson, Francis W. *Reminiscences of Confederate Service, 1861-1865.* Ed. by Bell Irvin Wiley. Baton Rouge: Louisiana State University Press, 1980.

Drake, George. *The Mail Goes Through, or The Civil War Letters of George Drake (1846-1918): Over Eighty Letters Written from August 9, 1862 to May 29, 1865 by 85th Illinois Vol.* Comp. and ed. by Julia A. Drake. San Angelo, Tex.: Anchor Publishing, 1964.

Dwight, Wilder. *Life and Letters of Wilder Dwight.* Boston: Ticknor & Fields, 1868.

Free at Last: A Documentary History of Slavery, Freedom, and the Civil War. Ed. by Ira Berlin, et al. New York: New Press, 1992.

Giles, Val C. *Rags and Hope: The Recollections of Val C. Giles, Four Years with Hood's Brigade, Fourth Texas Infantry, 1861-1865.* Comp. and ed. by Mary Lasswell. New York: Coward-McCann, 1961.

Goodloe, Albert Theodore. *Some Rebel Relics from the Seat of War.* Nashville: Publishing House of the Methodist Episcopal Church, 1893.

Grisamore, Silas T. *The Civil War Reminiscences of Major Silas T. Grisamore, C.S.A.* Baton Rouge: Louisiana State University Press, 1993.

Handerson, Henry E. *Yankee in Gray: The Civil War Memoirs of Henry E. Handerson.* [Cleveland]: Press of Western Reserve University, 1962.

Haydon, Charles B. *For Country, Cause & Leader: The Civil War Journal of Charles B. Haydon.* Ed. by Stephen W. Sears. New York: Ticknor & Fields, 1993.

Hermann, Isaac. *Memoirs of a Veteran.* Lakemont, Ga.: CSA Press, 1974.

Hinman, Wilbur F. *Corporal Si Klegg and His "Pard."* Cleveland: N. G. Hamilton, 1889.

Hitchcock, Frederick L. *War from the Inside: The Story of the 132nd Regiment Pennsylvania Volunteer Infantry in the War for the Suppression of the Rebellion, 1862-1863.* Philadelphia: Press of J. B. Lippincott, 1904.

Holt, Daniel M. *A Surgeon's Civil War: The Letters and Diary of Daniel M. Holt, M.D.* Ed. by James M. Greiner, Janet L. Coryell, and James R. Smither. Kent, Ohio: Kent State University Press, 1994.

Jamison, Robert D. *Letters and Recollections of a Confederate Soldier, 1860-1865.* Comp. by Henry Downs Jamison Jr. and Marguerite Jamison McTigue. Nashville: H. D. Jamison, 1964.

Johnston, David E. *The Story of a Confederate Boy in the Civil War.* Portland, Oreg.: Glass & Prudhomme, 1914.

Livermore, Thomas L. *Days and Events, 1860-1866.* Boston: Houghton Mifflin, 1920.

Lyman, Theodore. *Meade's Headquarters, 1863-1865: Letters of Colonel Theodore Lyman from the Wilderness to Appomattox.* Ed. by George R. Agassiz. Boston: Atlantic Monthly Press, 1922.

McCarthy, Carlton. *Detailed Minutiae of Soldier Life in the Army of Northern Virginia, 1861-1865.* Richmond: Carlton McCarthy, 1882.

Marvel, William, comp. *Biographical Sketches of the Contributors to the Military Order of the Loyal Legion of the United States.* Wilmington, N.C.: Broadfoot Publishing, 1995.

Moneyhon, Carl, and Bobby Roberts. *Portraits of Conflict: A Photographic History of Louisiana in the Civil War.* Fayetteville: University of Arkansas Press, 1990.

Mosman, Chesley A. *The Rough Side of War: The Civil War Journal of Chesley A. Mosman 1st Lieutenant, Company D 59th Illinois Volunteer Infantry Regiment.* Ed. by Arnold Gates. Garden City, N.Y.: Basin Publishing, 1987.

Nisbet, James Cooper. *Four Years on the Firing Line.* Ed. by Bell Irvin Wiley. Jackson, Tenn.: McCowat-Mercer Press, 1963.

Pardee, George K. *My Dear Carrie: The Civil War Letters of George K. Pardee and Family.* Ed. by Robert H. Jones. Akron: Summit County Historical Society Press, 1994.

Patrick, Robert. *Reluctant Rebel: The Secret Diary of Robert Patrick, 1861-1865.* Ed. by F. Jay Taylor. Baton Rouge: Louisiana State University Press, 1959.

Potter, John. *Reminiscences of the Civil War in the United States.* [Oskaloosa, Iowa]: Globe Presses, 1897.

Ramey, Emily G., and John K. Gott. *The Years of Anguish: Fauquier County, Virginia, 1861-1865.* Fauquier, Va.: Fauquier County Civil War Centennial Committee, 1965.

Richardson, George S. *"For My Country": The Richardson Letters, 1861-1865.* Comp. and ed. by Gordon C. Jones. Wendell, N.C.: Broadfoot Publishing, 1984.

Roberson, Elizabeth Whitley. *Weep Not for Me, Dear Mother.* Washington, N.C.: Venture Press, 1991.

Robertson, James I., Jr., and the Editors of Time-Life Books. *Tenting Tonight.* (The Civil War series). Alexandria, Va.: Time-Life Books, 1984.

Roth, Margaret Brobst, ed. *Well Mary: Civil War Letters of a Wisconsin Volunteer.* Madison: University of Wisconsin Press, 1960.

Scribner, B. F. *How Soldiers Were Made, or The War as I Saw It under Buell, Rosecrans, Thomas, Grant and Sherman.* Huntington, W.Va.: Blue Acorn Press, 1995 (reprint of 1887 edition).

Shotwell, Randolph Abbott. *The Papers of Randolph Abbott Shotwell,* Vol. 1. Ed. by J. G. de Roulhac Hamilton. Raleigh: North Carolina Historical Commission, 1929.

Shultz, John A., and Hobart L. Morris Jr. *One Year at War: The Diary of Private John A. Shultz, August 1, 1863-August 1, 1864.* New York: Vantage Press, 1968.

Sifakis, Stewart. *Who Was Who in the Civil War.* New York: Facts on File, 1988.

Simpson, R. W. *"Far, Far from Home": The Wartime Letters of Dick and Tally Simpson, Third South Carolina Volunteers.* Ed. by Guy R. Everson and Edward W. Simpson Jr. New York: Oxford University Press, 1994.

Small, Abner R. *The Road to Richmond: The Civil War Memoirs of Major Abner R. Small of the Sixteenth Maine Volunteers.* Ed. by Harold Adams Small. Berkeley: University of California Press, 1939.

Smedlund, William S. *Camp Fires of Georgia's Troops, 1861-1865.* [Lithonia, Ga.: William S. Smedlund], 1995.

Snetsinger, Robert J., comp. and ed. *Kiss Clara for Me: The Story of Joseph Whitney and His Family, Early Days in the Midwest, and Soldiering in the American Civil War.* State College, Pa.: Carnation Press, 1969.

Stevens, John W. *Reminiscences of the Civil War: A Soldier in Hood's Texas Brigade, Army of Northern Virginia.* Powhatan, Va.: Derwent Books, 1982 (reprint of 1902 edition).

Timerman, John D. *"Dear Wife": The Correspondence of John D. Timerman, 3rd New York Cavalry, to His Wife Mary, Dated September 1861 to October 1864.* N.p., 1987.

Trout, Robert J. *They Followed the Plume: The Story of J. E. B. Stuart and His Staff.* Mechanicsburg, Pa.: Stackpole Books, 1993.

United States War Department. *The War of the Rebellion,* 128 vols. Washington, D.C.: Government Printing Office, 1902.

Virdin, Donald Odell. *The Civil War Correspondence of Judge Thomas Goldsborough Odell.* Bowie, Md.: Heritage Books, 1992.

Vredenburgh, Peter. *Letters of Major Peter Vredenburgh . . . the Battles and Marches of the Old Fourteenth Regiment N.J. Vols. . . .* N.p.: Private printing, [187-].

Welch, Spencer Glasgow. *A Confederate Surgeon's Letters to His Wife.* Marietta, Ga.: Continental Book Co., 1954 (reprint of 1911 edition).

Weller, Edwin. *A Civil War Courtship: The Letters of Edwin Weller from Antietam to Atlanta.* Ed. by William Walton. Garden City, N.Y.: Doubleday, 1980.

Wiley, Bell Irvin:

The Life of Billy Yank: The Common Soldier of the Union. Baton Rouge: Louisiana State University Press, 1981.

The Life of Johnny Reb: The Common Soldier of the Confederacy. Baton Rouge: Louisiana State University Press, 1980.

PERIODICALS

Bartmess, Jacob W.:

"Jacob W. Bartmess Civil War Letters." Ed. by Donald E. Carmony. *Indiana Magazine of History,* March 1956.

"Jacob W. Bartmess Civil War Letters." Ed. by Donald E. Carmony. *Indiana Magazine of History,* June 1956.

Braxton, F. L. " 'Hooa, Hooa, Hooa.' " *National Tribune* (Washington, D.C.), March 7, 1895.

Brown, A. C. "Dog Soup." *National Tribune* (Washington, D.C.), July 22, 1896.

Coffin, Gorham. "Civil War Letters of Gorham Coffin." Ed. by Herbert A. Wisbey Jr. *Essex Institute Historical Collections,* January 1957.

Cooney, Charles F. "Engineers and Entertainment." *Civil War Times Illustrated,* November 1976.

Daniels, Isaac. "A Wash-Pot of Whiskey." *Augusta Herald,* October 11, 1896.

Eldredge, Daniel. "The Military History of Daniel Eldredge, Written by Himself." Ed. by John H. Lindenbusch. *Historical New Hampshire,* Winter 1964.

Frederick, John T. "Capturing a Skillet." *National Tribune* (Washington, D.C.), April 7, 1887.

"From the Army of the Potomac: Bold Attack on the First Regiment P.R.V.C." *Lancaster Daily Evening Express* (Pa.), March 29, 1864.

F. S. H. "A Sound of Revelry: A 'Light Fantastic' Reminiscence of the Second Corps." *National Tribune* (Washington, D.C.), April 21, 1887.

Greenalch, James. "Civil War Letters, 1862-1865." Ed. by Knox Mellon Jr. *Michigan History,* June 1960.

Hadley, John V. "An Indiana Soldier in Love and War: The Civil War Letters of John V. Hadley." Ed. by James I. Robertson Jr. *Indiana Magazine of History,* September 1963.

Harris, Loyd G. "Army Music." *National Tribune* (Washington, D.C.), June 19, 1902.

Haskell, C. C. "Raiding a Sutler's Tent." *National Tribune* (Washington, D.C.), May 8, 1902.

Jeffries, Lemuel. " 'The Excitement Had Begun!': The Civil War Diaries of Lemuel Jeffries, 1862-1863." Ed. by Jason H. Silverman. *Manuscripts,* Fall 1978.

Lang, John C. "Some Breezy Recollections of an Illinois Infantryman." *National Tribune* (Washington, D.C.), October 7, 1886.

Morris, A. "The Army Mail." *National Tribune* (Washington, D.C.), August 18, 1887.

O'Leary, Daniel. "The Civil War Letters of Captain Daniel O'Leary, U.S.A." Ed. by Jenny O'Leary and Harvey H. Jackson. *The Register of the Kentucky Historical Society,* Summer 1979.

Quenzel, Carrol H. "Johnny Bull—Billy Yank." *Tennessee Historical Quarterly,* June 1955.

Reichard, William J. "Civil War Letters of William J. Reichard, 1862-1863." *Proceedings of the Lehigh County Historical Society,* August 1958.

Ridley, Bromfield L. "B. L. Ridley's Journal." *Confederate Veteran,* 1895, Vol. 3.

Temple, Wayne C., ed. "A Chaplain in the 11th Missouri Infantry." *Lincoln Herald,* Summer 1962.

Worden, George H. "The Army Galoot." *National Tribune* (Washington, D.C.), March 28, 1895.

Yard, W. C. "Fighting Them Over." *National Tribune* (Washington, D.C.), October 22, 1896.

OTHER SOURCES

Goodwin, David George. Letters. Confederate Collection, Box 9, Folder 12. Columbia, Tenn.: James K. Polk Auxiliary, Civil War Collection: Confederate and Federal, 1861-1865.

Jarman, Robert A. "The History of Company K, 27th Mississippi Infantry, and Its First and Last Muster Rolls." Unpublished memoirs. Jackson: Mississippi Department of State Archives and History.

Johnson, Richard L. Letter, June 15, 1863. Johnson Family Papers. Charleston, S.C.: South Carolina Historical Society.

Kilpatrick, Madison. Letters, August-October 1864. Auburn, Ala.: Auburn University, Department of Archives.

McKenna, Charles F. Letter, March 18, 1864. Pittsburgh: Soldiers and Sailors Memorial Hall, Library.

Moffatt, Thomas William, Sr., and Wallace Wilson Moffatt. "A Union Soldier's Civil War." Unpublished manuscript, 1962. Montgomery: Alabama Department of Archives and History.

Orwig, Thomas G. Letter, March 14, 1863. Lewisburg, Pa.: Private Collection.

Rainey, Isaac Newton. "Experiences of I. N. Rainey in the Confederate Army." Memoirs, February 1925. Nashville: Tennessee State Library and Archives, Civil War Collection.

Smith, Anton. Pension Deposition. Pennsylvania State Adjutant Generals Records, Record Group 19. Harrisburg: Pennsylvania State Archives.

INDEX

VOICES OF THE CIVIL WAR

SERIES EDITOR: Henry Woodhead
Administrative Editor: Philip Brandt George
Picture Editor: Paula York-Soderlund

Editorial Staff for *Soldier Life*
Deputy Editor: Harris J. Andrews
Senior Art Director: Ray Ripper
Text Editor: John Newton
Associate Editors Research/Writing: Connie Contreras,
Kirk Denkler
Senior Copyeditor: Donna D. Carey
Picture Coordinator: Paige Henke
Editorial Assistant: Christine Higgins

Initial Series Design: Studio A

Special Contributors: Mark Galan, Brian C. Pohanka, Gerald P.
Tyson (text); Martha Lee Beckington, Patricia Cassidy,
Charles F. Cooney, Henry Mintz, Anne Whittle (research);
Roy Nanovic (index).

Correspondent: Christina Lieberman (New York).

Consultants
Brian C. Pohanka, a Civil War historian and author, spent six
years as a researcher and writer for Time-Life Books' Civil
War series and Echoes of Glory. He is the author of *Distant
Thunder: A Photographic Essay on the American Civil War* and
has written and edited numerous works on American military
history. He has acted as historical consultant for projects such
as the feature film *Glory* and television's *Civil War Journal*.
Pohanka participates in Civil War reenactments and living-
history demonstrations with the 5th New York Volunteers,
and he is active in Civil War battlefield preservation.

Les Jensen, a museum curator with the U.S. Department of
the Army, specializes in Civil War artifacts. He has worked
with numerous state, federal, and private museums and for
eight years was the curator of collections for the Museum of
the Confederacy in Richmond. Jensen has been a consultant
and contributor for numerous Civil War publications, including The Image of War series and Time-Life Books' Echoes
of Glory, and he is the author of the 32d Virginia Infantry volume in the Virginia Regimental Histories series.

Richard A. Sauers is a historian specializing in the Civil War.
As chief historian for the Pennsylvania Capitol Preservation
Committee, he directed the research and documentation of
more than 400 Civil War battle flags and wrote *Advance the
Colors!,* the two-volume study of Pennsylvania's Civil War
flags. He is active in Civil War and local historical societies and
is involved in battlefield preservation. He is assistant editor of
Gettysburg magazine. His published works include *A Caspian
Sea of Ink: The Meade-Sickles Controversy* and *"The Bloody 85th":
A Supplement to the History of the 85th Pennsylvania.*

Time-Life Books is a division of Time Life Inc.

PRESIDENT AND CEO: John M. Fahey Jr.

TIME-LIFE BOOKS

MANAGING EDITOR: Roberta Conlan

Director of Design: Michael Hentges
Editorial Production Manager: Ellen Robling
Director of Operations: Eileen Bradley
Director of Photography and Research: John Conrad Weiser
Senior Editors: Russell B. Adams Jr., Janet Cave, Lee Hassig,
Robert Somerville, Henry Woodhead
Library: Louise D. Forstall

PRESIDENT: John D. Hall

Vice President, Director of New Product Development: Neil Kagan
Associate Directors, New Product Development: Elizabeth D.
Ward, Curtis Kopf
Marketing Director: Pamela R. Farrell
Vice President, Book Production: Marjann Caldwell
Production Manager: Marlene Zack